NATURE WALKS ALONG THE SEACOAST

Massachusetts
New Hampshire
Maine

Julia Older and Steve Sherman

D1432346

APPALACHIAN MOUNTAIN CLUB BOOKS
BOSTON, MASSACHUSETTS

Cover Photograph: Jerry and Marcy Monkman
All photographs by the authors unless otherwise noted.
Cover Design: Victoria Sax and Brandy Polay
Book & Map Design: Carol Bast Tyler

Library of Congress Cataloging-in-Publication Data

Older, Julia, 1941-
  Nature walks along the seacoast : Massachusetts, New Hampshire, Maine
/ Julia Older and Steve Sherman.
    p. cm.
  ISBN 1-929173-12-1
  1. Hiking—Atlantic Coast (New England)—Guidebooks. 2. Nature
trails—Atlantic Coast (New England)—Guidebooks. 3. Atlantic Coast
(New England)—Guidebooks. I. Sherman, Steve, 1938- II. Title.
GV199.42.A83 A53 2003
917.4044—dc21

                                                          2003001113

The paper used in this publication meets the minimum requirements of the
American National Standard for Information Sciences—Permanence of
Paper for Printed Library Materials, ANSI Z39.48–1984.∞

**Due to changes in conditions,
use of the information in this book
is at the sole risk of the user.**

⊕ Printed on recycled paper using soy-based inks.

Printed in the United States of America.

10 9 8 7 6 5 4 3 2 1   03 04 05 06 07 08 09

Contents

New Hampshire

Maine

Introduction

The northern Atlantic seacoast contains an extraordinary array of seascapes, landscapes, and walking escapes from daily routines. These fifty-one trails are located on 60 miles of seacoast—as the gull flies—from Ipswich, Massachusetts, to the Kennebunks in Maine. They're situated in an area up to about 10 miles inland, which includes Great Bay of New Hampshire. The trails are accessible by I-95, coastal US 1, and state roads. Most walks are an easy 1 or 2 miles round-trip.

Although the New England coast was formed by glacial activity during the ice ages, what's fascinating is that each state has singular geological and climatic features. Differences in microclimates and water temperatures produce an intriguing variety of flora and fauna. The walks begin with sand dunes in Massachusetts and end with the rocky inlets of Maine. This lay of the land engenders indicator species of plants and marine life adapted to each area.

Near Boston, formal gardens and estates flourished during the golden age of industrial wealth. New Hampshire developed Portsmouth, one of the nations largest, most strategic working ports, while in Maine emphasis was on fishing and farming, rocky coves and inlets. For example, at Castle Hill in Massachusetts, you walk the estate grounds with an overlook of a 4,000-acre preserve managed by The Trustees of Reservations. In historic Portsmouth, New Hampshire, you cross the busy Piscataqua River and watch international tankers and tugboats near the Portsmouth Naval Shipyard. In Maine, small-town land trusts allow you to walk wilderness areas such as Tyler Brook and Vaughn Island Preserves.

The Turf of Surf

All three states encompass sand dunes, barrier beaches, mud flats, estuary marshes, and other tidal features. In Massachusetts, you'll walk sections of one of the largest estuaries on the northern seaboard—25,000 acres. In New Hampshire, several walks offer different perspectives of 10,000-acre Great Bay, and in Maine, two trails are in Rachel Carson National Wildlife Refuge, bordering the 160,000 acres of the Gulf of Maine.

An estuary is a wetland where fresh river water and ocean salt water meet. This confluence forms a nutrient-rich ecosystem for marine life on a floodplain of marsh grass and mud flats. Because of the ebb and flow of the tides, many of the outings are on boardwalks to keep your feet dry and protect these important, fragile environments.

Major tidal rivers include the Merrimack and Ipswich Rivers in Massachusetts; Piscataqua, Lamprey, Oyster, and Squamscott Rivers in New Hampshire; and York, Webhannet, Little, and Ogunquit Rivers in Maine.

You'll also be walking through upland seaside meadows and inland sand plains, along harbor jetties and riverbanks, in white pine forests and shagbark hickory groves, up a coastal drumlin and a mountain, and even on two islands.

Marine Life

The biodiversity of seashore life is fascinating—from tube worms to kelp, jellyfish to bluefish, jingle shells to lobster shells. In a coastal forest, you might spot a white-tailed deer or otter. In a salt marsh, look for great blue herons and green crabs. Mud flats are home to lesser yellowlegs and 2-foot-long clam worms, tidal inlets nourish oysters and ducks, and rocky shores are feeding and spawning grounds for seals and cormorants.

Tides bring in flotsam and jetsam for closer observations and also leave behind tide pools. These mirrorlike pools reflect a colorful microcosmos of the ocean—periwinkles, brine shrimp, crabs, and scuds. The tide line is composed of a wealth of discoveries—finger sponges, crab shells, blue mussel shells, skate egg packets, kelp, and much more.

Walking with Children

Children are closer to the ground than adults. They love to beachcomb but might stick little objects of nature in their mouths. To avoid this compulsive tasting, bring along plastic bags for them to carry their sea treasures home in for later examination.

Children have shorter legs and expend a lot of energy. To keep them going, pack plenty of high-energy snacks—raisins, cookies—and rest frequently. Take your time. In the woods, find them kid-size walking sticks. Near water, be sure to hold their hands. Remember that children sunburn easily; carry sunscreen and hats.

School-age children might especially enjoy the following trails:

- Rockery Trail (Ipswich, Massachusetts)
- Hellcat Dunes Trail (Newburyport, Massachusetts)
- Ocean and River Trail (Salisbury Beach, Massachusetts)
- Odiorne Point Trail (Rye, New Hampshire)
- Sandy Point Discovery Center Identification Trail and wigwam site (Greenland/Stratham, New Hampshire)

- Fort Trail, Fort McClary (Kittery, Maine)
- Wiggly Bridge (York, Maine)
- Nubble Trail and Lighthouse (York, Maine)

Seasons

Many of the trail sites include visitor centers with exhibits explaining the seacoast environment and ecology. The formal season for these sites is from the beginning of June to the beginning of September. When in doubt, find out—call ahead. Nevertheless, although welcome centers may be closed in spring and fall, you usually can find pass-through gates for off-season access.

Some sites charge for historical tours but allow visitors to walk the grounds and trails gratis. For the few sites that do charge fees, the cost is nominal. One exception is the Isles of Shoals, which charges for the ferry crossing.

Walking in spring and fall has its advantages—less road traffic and fewer people on the trails. Early spring may be soggy in some locations, but blackflies are nonexistent. Spring warblers use the coast as a flyway; wildflowers flourish in the moist seacoast woods and marshes. In fall the coast is cool and dry. Monarch butterflies and geese migrate south. Dragonflies are easier to spot. With the foliage gone, you have deeper visibility into the woodlands. And one bright October day, we counted a dozen harbor seals right offshore.

Walking and Gawking

Let's face it, the seacoast is photogenic—Nubble Light, Fort McClary, beach roses on the Isles of Shoals, sailboats off Plum Island. Bring your camera and plenty of film.

Also, bring along binoculars. We use compact binoculars that weigh little and are powerful. The more compact, the better. Hang them on your neck and out of the way. Binoculars are wonderful for watching lobstermen hauling in their pots or focusing on rare piping plovers and dragonflies close up.

We also travel with a small portable library of nature identification guides for seashore outings (one of our favorites is *The Seaside Naturalist* by Deborah A. Coulombe).

How to Prepare and What to Wear

Feet First: If you're on a beach or mud flat, wear rubber-soled beach sandals. If you're on a boardwalk in an estuary near tidewater edge forest, wear rubber-soled sneakers or boots.

Socks Second: Deer nest in coastal areas and carry microscopic ticks, which can transmit Lyme disease during a certain stage of their development. To protect yourself from all ticks, pull socks over the cuffs of long, light-colored jeans (larger ticks are more easily spotted on light-colored clothing). If you spot a circular welt or rash on your skin or develop a fever after walking on the seacoast, immediately see a physician.

Hat Third: Many of these walks are in the open on the beach. A hat protects you from heatstroke and harmful sun rays. A hat also keeps ticks from dropping on your head. (At Plum Island, a visible tick from one of the plum tree branches dropped on our notebook.)

Another handy item at the seashore is a nylon windbreaker with a hood. Windbreakers are lightweight, mosquito proof, and rain/wind resistant. You may spread them on a rock or beach to sit on. Deep pockets are useful for carrying a small water bottle, sunscreen, and binoculars. If you don't want to bring a windbreaker, a hip pack can accommodate these items.

The seacoast has "water water everywhere and not a drop to drink." Be sure to take along bottles of fresh water even on shorter trails. While hiking the Appalachian Trail, we learned how quickly you can get dehydrated walking in the hot sun. A swallow or two of water on your walk refreshes body and spirit. Pocket-size cartons of juices also are great thirst quenchers.

Seacoast Nature Walks offers a variety of appealing alternatives to beach basking. On cooler days vacationing families can visit ecocenters with marine pools and exhibits, and on blistering hot days they can enjoy shady, wooded walks. Older couples staying in resort towns can take leisurely strolls at their own pace. Power walkers can climb a drumlin or a mountain. Historical monuments and sites add an extra dimension to many of the walks.

On these seaside outings, mundane problems seem to slip away. We hope you experience carefree and calm moments, as we have, and return to your everyday life refreshed and renewed.

Trip Highlights Chart

Location	Walk	Page	Miles	Difficulty
Mass.	Observation Tower Trail	1	1.0	Easy
	Rockery Trail	7	1.25	Moderate
	Pingree Forest Trail	12	1.8	Moderate
	Cedar Point Trail	17	2.0	Moderate
	Great House Formal Gardens and Estate Trail	22	1.7–2.0	Moderate
	Pines Trail	28	0.3	Easy
	Hellcat Freshwater Marsh Trail	32	0.7	Moderate
	Hellcat Dunes Trail	37	0.6	Moderate
	Eliza Little Walking Trail	42	1.0	Easy
	Drumlin Trail	47	1.3	Moderate
	River and Pond Trail	52	1.6	Moderate
	Hedge Drive Trail	58	1.5	Moderate
	Ocean and River Trail	63	0.75	Moderate
N.H.	Hickory Trail	69	1.25	Moderate
	Ragged Neck Trail	74	0.5	Easy
	Star Island Shore Trail	80	1.75	Moderate

Fee	Beach	Vista	Visitor Center	Wetland Pond	River	Woods
✔		✔	✔	✔	✔	✔
✔			✔	✔	✔	✔
✔			✔	✔	✔	✔
✔	✔	✔				✔
✔		✔		✔		✔
✔		✔		✔		✔
✔	✔	✔		✔		✔
			✔	✔		
	✔					✔
		✔	✔	✔	✔	✔
	✔	✔				✔
✔	✔	✔			✔	
				✔		✔
✔	✔	✔	✔			
✔	✔	✔	✔			

Fee	Beach	Vista	Visitor Center	Wetland Pond	River	Woods
✔			✔			
✔	✔	✔	✔			
		✔	✔	✔		✔
		✔			✔	
		✔	✔	✔		✔
		✔			✔	
		✔			✔	✔
		✔	✔	✔		✔
	✔	✔	✔	✔		✔
	✔	✔		✔		✔
		✔	✔	✔		✔
			✔	✔		✔
		✔		✔	✔	✔
✔	✔	✔			✔	
✔	✔	✔		✔	✔	✔
	✔	✔			✔	✔
		✔			✔	
		✔	✔	✔		

Fee	Beach	Vista	Visitor Center	Wetland Pond	River	Woods
		✔				✔
		✔	✔		✔	✔
		✔	✔			
	✔	✔			✔	
		✔	✔			
✔		✔	✔	✔	✔	✔
✔		✔	✔			✔
✔		✔	✔	✔	✔	✔
			✔	✔		
			✔			
		✔		✔	✔	✔
		✔		✔	✔	✔
		✔	✔			
	✔	✔	✔	✔	✔	
✔	✔			✔		
✔	✔		✔	✔		
			✔	✔	✔	

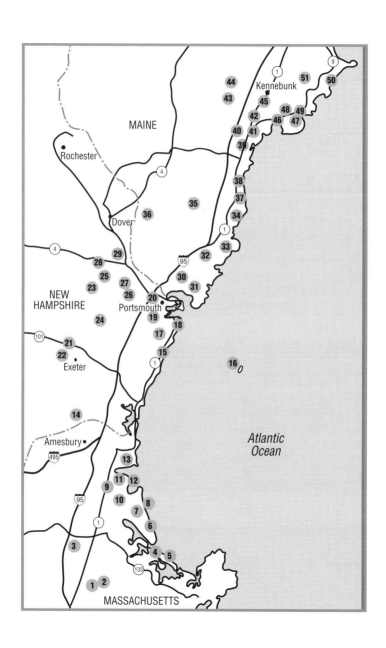

Locator Map

Massachusetts

New Hampshire

Maine

Observation Tower Trail

Ipswich River Wildlife Sanctuary (2,800 acres)

Topsfield, Massachusetts

Distance: 1.0 mile
Type of walk: Loop
Approximate time: 1 hour
Difficulty: Easy

*Varied landscape including woods, geological features, meadow
and river habitats, and a view of Great Wenham Swamp.*

Getting There

From the fire station in Topsfield, drive south on MA 97 for 1.1
miles. At the Audubon sign, turn left onto Perkins Row (the
Perkins Row street sign may be obscured partially by tree
branches). Drive 1.0 mile to the Ipswich River Wildlife Sanctuary. Parking is available 0.3 mile past the sign.

Special Features
- Glacial drumlin and eskers
- High observation deck overlooking Great Wenham Swamp
- Exhibits, educational programs, gift shop

At 2,800 acres, the Ipswich River Wildlife Sanctuary is the
largest Audubon site in Massachusetts, with 8 miles of the

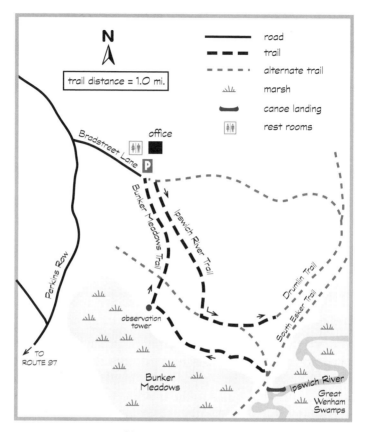

Observation Tower Trail

Ipswich River winding through the sanctuary. The Ipswich River starts 30 miles inland, snakes through Great Wenham Swamp, and eventually empties into the Atlantic Ocean.

The Ipswich River Trail begins directly opposite the Audubon sanctuary office and staff residence, a large house on Bradstreet Lane built by one of Governor Bradstreet's grandsons in 1763.

The Audubon offices and resource center complex are located on top of a drumlin formed approximately 15,000 years ago when a glacial ice sheet covered this land. As the mile-thick glaciers melted, deposits of sand, silt, clay, and other sediments formed low hills—drumlins—around what is now greater Boston.

During this same period of glaciation, creeks flowed beneath the ice sheet, forming banks of sediment called eskers such as this walk's South Esker. Glacial erratics (large, freestanding boulders) were dumped in this area during this time.

Heading south from the trailhead, follow the mowed green swath along the edge of a meadow with bluebird boxes and other bird shelters. You might hear the bobolink's cheery song bubbling upward. You can easily spot the males in their tuxedo-like plumage (white on top, black below); females are more sparrowlike. American kestrels also can be seen hunting for prey in the meadow.

Following a gradual downhill slope, in 0.2 mile you come to the Drumlin Trail intersection encircling the base of the drumlin. Turn left onto the Drumlin Trail. At 0.3 mile is an arbor on the right that once probably supported grapes but now is a tangle of wild vines.

Turn right just past the arbor onto an unmarked dirt path at a tumble of stones; if you miss it, a second narrow path a few yards farther on the right will do. The path makes a shortcut through forest to the South Esker Trail. Turn right onto the

The three-story Bunker Meadows Observation Tower overlooks a broad expanse of Great Wenham Swamp.

South Esker Trail and walk the esker, a long, narrow ridge of glacial sediment resembling a railroad embankment.

A hundred yards south of the South Esker Trail is a canoe landing on a sandy stretch of shore on the Ipswich River. (The canoes kept here are for the use of Audubon members only.)

The river is stained a dark tea color by tannins leaching into the water from swamp maple foliage, roots, peat, and other vegetation. A swamp is a forest with wet feet. Indicator species include speckled alder, buttonbush, and red and black swamp maple. River otter, mink, and muskrat make their homes on Candlewood Island, Pine Island, and other islands in the swamp and swim through the dense growth.

At the canoe landing opposite the South Esker Trail, turn left onto the Bunker Meadows Trail. At 0.6 mile stands a giant sycamore tree with its typical mottled beige, green, and brown trunk. Along with willows, sycamores grow near rivers and other freshwater sources. Another water-loving plant, wild grape, grows here. Look high in the tree canopy for its woody vines and large maple-shaped leaves. These wild grapes probably originated at the arbor you passed earlier and now proliferate closer to the swamp.

Walk through a red maple grove, and at 0.8 mile you'll arrive at the thirty-two-step, three-story Bunker Meadows Observation Tower. Before you climb the tower, notice on the right side of the trail a strangler tree twisting around another tree as it reaches for sunlight.

The strong platform observation tower may sway in the breeze slightly, but if you're a birder this is the place to be. In spring and early summer, the meadow is full of the *clucking* and *trilling* of red-winged blackbirds. Tree and barn swallows swoop for mosquitoes (which, fortunately, are left behind the higher you climb). We startled a pair of Baltimore orioles, their bright orange-and-black plumage flashing in the buttonbush below.

Buttonbush thrives along the Atlantic Ocean in swampy areas. It has ball-shaped, fragrant white blossoms that turn brown in fall, 4- to 7-inch leaves, and can grow to 30 feet. This tree is one of 6,000 species in the Madder family, including tropical species such as coffee, cinchonas (quinine), and gardenia.

From the tower you can often see great blue herons and egrets flying over the expansive meadows and willow fronds swaying in the breeze.

Back on the Bunker Meadows Trail, gradually ascend and cross the Drumlin Trail at 0.9 mile, walking along the stepped path next to a stone wall on your left.

This mile-long trail ends back at the Audubon office.

Hours, Fees, and Facilities
Hours of operation vary seasonally. The sanctuary is free to Audubon members; otherwise, adults pay $3, children and seniors $2.

For More Information
Ipswich River Audubon Wildlife Sanctuary, 87 Perkins Row, Topsfield, MA 01983; 978-887-9264; ipswichriver:massaudubon.org; www.massaudubon.org.

Rockery Trail

Ipswich River Wildlife Sanctuary (2,800 acres)

Topsfield, Massachusetts

Trip 2

Distance: **1.25 miles**
Type of walk: **Out-and-back with a loop**
Approximate time: **1 hour**
Difficulty: **Moderate**

Descend from a drumlin field through swamp habitats to a pond and enchanting rock garden.

Getting There

From the fire station in Topsfield, drive south on MA 97 for 1.1 miles. At the Audubon sign, turn left onto Perkins Row (the Perkins Row street sign may be obscured partially by tree branches). Drive 1.0 mile to the sign for Ipswich River Wildlife Sanctuary. Parking is available 0.3 mile past the sign.

Special Features

• Audubon bird observatory and program center
• Fantastic rock garden and grotto
• Marsh boardwalk

The Rockery Trail begins at the edge of a grassy field next to the Audubon offices and resource center complex, which sits on a

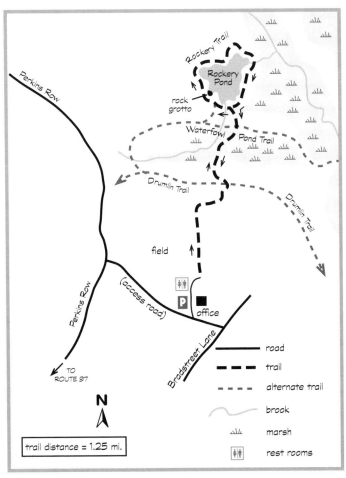

Rockery Trail

drumlin. All trails at the sanctuary descend this hill formed of mineral deposits left by glaciers of the last ice age, 15,000 years ago (see walk 1).

The mowed swath takes you north across a field with many poled birdhouses. Bluebirds nest here in spring. Like robins, bluebirds belong to the Thrush family but are more the size of sparrows, with eye-catching blue backs and rust-colored breasts. In the low-growing thickets, you might spot a squat, brown woodcock, known by its long needle-shaped bill.

Butterflies too abound, including the regal monarch with veined orange wings outlined with black and the common fritillaries with black spots and bars against orange wings. Monarchs feed and breed on the many milkweed plants growing in the field, and at least forty-two other butterfly species have been identified here.

Another insect that likes the sun is the common white-tailed dragonfly. Watch for these speedy, four-winged insects both near the entrance field and all along this walk, which leads you through a marsh and around a pond. Dragonflies are born in still water and stay near ponds and streams like these as they defend up to 180 square yards of territory. The presence of dragonflies is an indicator of a healthy wetland.

The Rockery Trail is wide and in less than 300 yards from the trailhead enters the woods. Notice the blue spruce on the right as you begin descending northeast toward the Drumlin Trail. More silvery gray than blue, the non-native blue spruce with short, prickly needles was introduced to New England from its native Rocky Mountain region as an ornamental tree.

Continuing downhill, the Rockery Trail crosses the Drumlin Trail. The trails are well marked, but stay alert to uneven footing created by tree roots. At 0.2 mile, a boardwalk takes you over a marsh. Look for the giant-leaved, smelly skunk cabbage, used by Abenaki Eastern natives to relieve asthma. In the mid-1800s the U.S. *Pharmacopoeia* listed the roots of this plant as an aid for respiratory and nervous disorders.

Cross the Waterfowl Pond Trail and continue straight ahead on the boardwalk, watching for clumps of purple loosestrife, with its needle-thin leaves and spiked magenta blossoms. This non-native invasive plant is a destructive, marsh-clogging species. Giant cattails are putting up a good territorial resistance while providing habitat for red-winged blackbirds.

At 0.3 mile, the Rockery Trail makes a Y junction as it loops around Rockery Pond. Turn left at this junction, following the trail as it descends to the water's edge. Cross the bridge and veer right along the shore of Rockery Pond.

A short distance farther on the left is the Rock Grotto, which consists of a rock tunnel narrow and high enough to

The exotic Rockery Trail crosses a footbridge and passes tropical plantings, including Amur corktree and miniature Alberta spruce.

walk through without bending, and a lookout above the tunnel. Beware of bats as you move through the tunnel. Turn left and climb stone steps to a rock platform surrounded by rhododendron, Japanese maple, Amur cork tree, dwarf Alberta spruce (which grows only to 10 feet high), and other ornamentals. Created by Thomas Proctor in the early 1900s, the Rockery was constructed with glacier boulders from nearby towns and numerous horticultural plantings.

Continue left around the edge of the pond, crossing a footbridge at pond level again. The pond has a primeval quality, and at openings on the loop you may see a heron, kingfisher, or other freshwater bird. A picturesque red footbridge arches across one end of the pond. At 0.75 mile as you curve around the pond to the right, the boardwalk leads to a short, junglelike rhododendron tunnel opening to the red bridge and a swampy area filled with cattails. Dragonflies and bluebottles zip here and there over the water.

You'll pass on the right a moss sawara false cypress with feathery gray-blue foliage, a native of Japan. A blanket of pine needles on the trail provides a cushion on this section of the walk.

After completing the pond loop at 1.0 mile, turn left at the junction and return to the trailhead.

Hours, Fees, and Facilities
Hours of operation vary seasonally. The sanctuary is free to Audubon members; adults pay $3, children and seniors $2.

For More Information
Ipswich River Audubon Wildlife Sanctuary, 87 Perkins Row, Topsfield, MA 01983; 978-887-9264; ipswichriver@massaudubon.org; www.massaudubon.org.

Pingree Forest Trail

Georgetown-Rowley State Forest (1,200 acres)

Georgetown, Massachusetts

Distance: **1.8 miles**
Type of walk: **Loop**
Approximate time: **1½ hours**
Difficulty: **Moderate**

A hardwood forest of maple, oak, and hickory near a residential area, providing year-round recreation.

Getting There

In Georgetown, at the intersection of MA 133 and 97, turn south onto MA 97 and drive 1.6 miles. Turn left onto Pingree Farm Road and drive 0.5 mile to the Georgetown-Rowley State Forest parking lot area at the gate. Pingree Farm Road continues but is gated to vehicular traffic beyond this point.

Special Features

- Woodland birds and flowers
- Closed to motorized recreation vehicles
- Mature hardwood forests

The trailhead begins at the gate to the right and behind the Georgetown-Rowley State Forest kiosk. On this walk, avoid the smaller paths that cut into the main trail. Oaks, white pines,

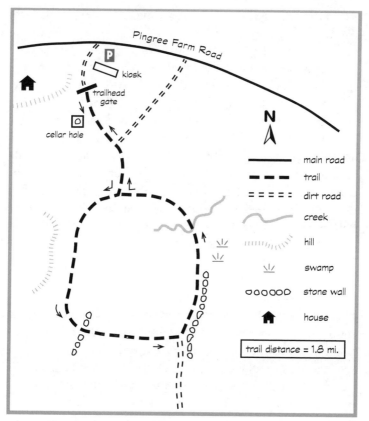

Pingree Forest Trail

and a few shagbark hickories of 80 to 90 feet leave the impression this forest has been in existence since the founding of Georgetown. In about 300 yards, to the right of the trail near a white birch, is a cellar hole bearing witness to earlier inhabitants in this area.

Farther along the trail, low-growing pipsissewa plants, with five to seven shiny, green, toothed leaves, grow in the verdant mosses on the forest floor. A few yards later, the dirt road veers right at a pair of double white blazes. This is the first of two right turns you will make on this loop. Although motorbikes have been prohibited recently, deep tire ruts filled with water are usually in evidence in spring. These puddles attract spring azure butterflies, which congregate to drink the dried minerals at the edge. This "puddling" is primarily a male thing. Salt, amino acids, and other essentials in the nutrient-rich mud are required by male azures to produce the sex pheremones that draw females. These nutrients are passed on to the female to help her produce healthy eggs. In summer when road puddles dry out, males can produce spit to mix with the dust to prepare for second matings.

Eastern tailed blues and spring azures belong to the same glittering, iridescent "gossamer family" of butterflies (Lycaenidae). However, small Eastern blues winter over as pupae, whereas spring azures hatch from eggs as larvae. After their transformation into butterflies, both species spiral and mate near pools like these, feeding on clover, vetch, and other woodland plants.

At about 0.25 mile in a swampy area, skunk cabbage and marsh marigolds flourish in spring. Marsh marigolds are actually large, water-loving buttercups. The purple mottled hoods of skunk cabbage poke up in early spring; then, in summer, huge leaves appear. A member of the Arum family, the malodorous plant was once used by Maine Micmac Indians, who inhaled crushed leaves to cure headache.

In a few yards is a second pair of white blazes and the beginning of the 1-mile loop. Keep right and ascend the rock-studded wide path through the woods.

Many common northern birds live in this forest—you'll hear the *squawking* of jays, the *chirring* of nuthatches, the high, sweet two-note call of chickadees, and the sad low *cooing* of the mourning doves.

At 0.5 mile, you'll pass through an opening in a stone wall to a carpet of white pine needles. Pass a rock outcrop on the right in another few hundred yards and gradually climb through smaller hardwoods on top of a knoll.

In this part of the forest, several snags (dead trees) provide food and lodging for smaller forest creatures. Woodpeckers drill into the rotting wood for insects, and red squirrels and chipmunks take refuge in the shelter of hollow trunks.

These marsh marigolds, a species of water-loving buttercup, thrive in early spring at Georgetown-Rowley State Forest.

At 0.8 mile, just beyond the knoll, is a towering white pine. Pines have shallow roots, and this one has stretched its roots over the path. Watch your step as you negotiate them and descend to a T junction abutting a stone wall. Turn left at the double white blaze. You're now heading back around the other side of the loop. The stone wall parallels the road and will be on your right.

In a few yards more, an extensive swamp spills over the road in spring. This is a good place to stop and to look. We saw a titmouse (a small, gray, wide-eyed bird with a crest) disappear into the hole of a snag to dine on a butterfly and spotted a red-tailed hawk circling overhead.

The roadbed turns sandy, and hardwoods give way to smaller trees that thrive in poor soil. The canopy is more open through a stand of white and gray birches, alders, and juniper bushes.

At 1.3 miles, another low, wet area may spill over the road. A few stepping stones will help you get across. Fiddlehead ferns poke up through the leaves, and marsh marigolds blaze bright gold among the leafy skunk cabbage. A creek crosses the road at 1.5 miles, and you soon return to the start of the loop. Make sure to veer right on the wide path with both white and yellow blazes (going left would take you back around the loop).

Now you're back on the dirt access road to the loop—this time with the cellar hole on your left. At 1.7 miles, the semi-circular path to Pingree Farm Road cuts in on the right. Keep left and at 1.8 miles return to the trailhead gate.

Cedar Point Trail

The Crane Reservation at Castle Hill (165 acres)

Ipswich, Massachusetts

Trip 4

Distance: **2.0 miles**
Type of walk: **Out-and-back**
Approximate time: **1½ hours**
Difficulty: **Moderate**

Wide-open views along a ridge road down to an extensive salt marsh at the mouth of Ipswich River and over white sand dunes to the Atlantic Ocean.

Getting There

From the Visitor Center in downtown Ipswich, turn south on MA 133 and drive 0.2 mile to Argilla Road. Turn left and drive 4.0 miles to the Castle Hill Crane Reservation sign and tollbooth on the left (fee required). (Argilla Road continues to the Crane Reservation Public Beach.) The well-marked public parking lot is to the left; the Castle Hill Inn lot is reserved for guests.

Special Features
• Wide, accessible dirt roads
• Fox Creek estuary
• A white sand beach
• Sand dunes

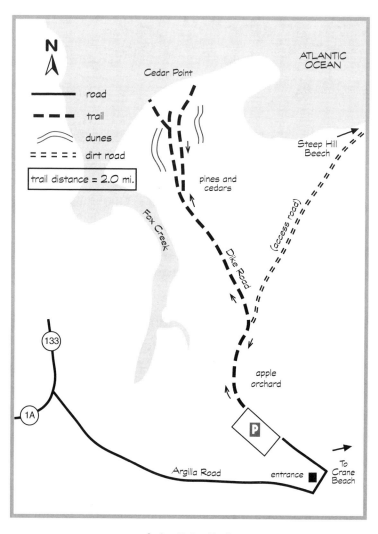

Cedar Point Trail

The first half of this walk gives you an overview of an immense estuary on Fox Creek, draining into the Atlantic Ocean; on the second half, you walk at eye level along the border of the same marsh. There is little shade, so sun protection is a good idea. At the outset keep alert for poison ivy, which favors sunny edges of open country roads, growing as a vine with three shiny, smooth leaves to a cluster. (See walk 5 for a description of Castle Hill and the Crane Estate.)

The Cedar Point Trail begins at a metal-bar gate at the back of the parking lot and follows a two-rut dirt road that runs along the edge of Castle Hill. Look for pink beach roses, red raspberries, and sumac. You'll also see purple loosestrife, a non-native (and, unfortunately, invasive) plant. Loosestrife nectar is relished by the common cabbage butterfly, easily identified by its white wings with one (male) or two (female) black dots.

After passing a stand of white pines on the left, you'll notice some grapevines, with their broad, maple-like leaves. In summer, green globes appear and grow larger as the warm season progresses.

The trail levels and curves slightly to the right at 0.2 mile and overlooks more of the tidal marsh. Across the Ipswich River, you'll see a cluster of Victorian summer cottages on a distant hill, a scene reminiscent of a bygone era.

At 0.3 mile, veer left at a **Y** junction onto Dike Road (the path to the right goes toward Steep Hill Beach). Descending a gentle slope, pass by a few old crab apple trees along the estuarine marsh.

Salt marshes and tidal rivers are highly important, dynamic environments for marine animal and plant life. These vast areas of ebb and flow are rich in nutrients from two types of spartina grass—salt marsh grass and salt meadow grass. Both

The final steps of Cedar Point Trail leads through protected sand dunes and fragile grasses to a secluded beach.

proliferate in the Fox Creek estuary. Cattails (also known as club rushes and reed mace) in the marsh are identified by their brown, fuzzy, hot-dog-like seed-bearing fruits. Cattail roots are edible and especially enjoyed by muskrats (marsh rabbits). This marsh is very active in spring with red-winged blackbirds perched on cattail stalks, staking out their territorial claims for mating.

Continue along Dike Road, with marshland now on both sides. At 0.75 mile, you'll reach a small section of sand dunes with a scattering of white Atlantic cedars, Scotch pine (good shade), and a "slat board" walkway up and over the dunes. On your left, where the Ipswich River meets the Atlantic, is a small boat harbor—a tranquil scene of white sand and clouds, blue water and sky.

At 0.9 mile, veer right at a Y junction into a head-high depression between sand dunes and follow the single-wire fence and boardwalk used to protect the fragile flora and nesting terns and plovers on the dunes. At 1.0 mile, you reach the private Steep Hill Beach at the mouth of Fox Creek and the end of the trail. Return the same way.

Hours, Fees, and Facilities

The trails are open from 9:00 A.M. to sunset. A fee of $5 per car is charged.

For More Information

The Crane Estate, 209 Argilla Road, Ipswich, MA 01938; 978-356-4351.

Great House Formal Gardens and Estate Trail

The Crane Reservation at Castle Hill (165 acres)

Ipswich, Massachusetts

Distance: 1.7–2.0 miles
Type of walk: **Loop**
Approximate time: **1–1½ hours**
Difficulty: **Moderate**

Turn-of-the-twentieth-century Italianate formal gardens of the Great House on Castle Hill.

Getting There

From the Visitor Center in downtown Ipswich, turn south on MA 133 and drive 0.2 mile to Argilla Road. Turn left and drive 4.0 miles to the Castle Hill Crane Reservation sign and toll-booth on the left (fee required). (Argilla Road continues to the Crane Reservation Public Beach.) The well-marked public parking lot is to the left; the Castle Hill Inn lot is reserved for guests.

Special Features

- Walled 1919 "secret" garden
- Sunken rose garden
- Magnificent central Grand Allée

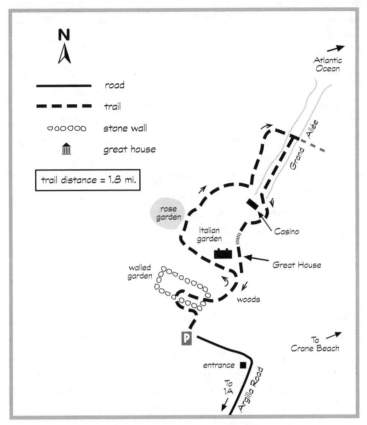

Great House Formal Gardens and Estate Trail

Once a working saltwater farm, a gentleman farmer purchased this property in the nineteenth century, naming it Castle Hill. Later his son inherited Castle Hill and began improvements to the buildings; he also enhanced the property's natural features.

In 1910, Richard T. Crane Jr. purchased the estate and built an Italianate villa-style mansion. The Chicago industrialist and manufacturer made his fortune on bathroom fixtures at a time when outhouses were being abandoned for indoor plumbing. Crane hired the Olmsted Brothers and Arthur Shurcliff to design the dramatic landscape and took on scores of gardeners to plant thousands of trees, shrubs, and plants. Today, three full-time gardeners and a dozen groundskeepers maintain 165-acre Castle Hill, a National Historical Landmark. Although you can imagine the original beauty of these gardens, their glory belongs to another era.

Castle Hill, Crane Wildlife Refuge, and Crane Beach comprise the 2,100-acre Crane Estate, now owned and managed by The Trustees of Reservations, a member-supported, Massachusetts-based conservation organization. In the summer months, Castle Hill is often crowded with private and public functions in the gardens and Great House. An especially nice, and less crowded, time for walking at Castle Hill is in fall when the leaves turn.

The trail to the formal gardens begins at a mowed path at the end of the parking lot nearest the carriage houses. At the top of the steep embankment, turn left and walk a few yards with a high stone wall on your right until you come to the entrance to a "secret" garden.

This rectangular walled garden with octagonal towers at each end was the estate's vegetable garden for the five summer weeks the Crane family was in residence at Castle Hill. Although the enclosure was probably meant to keep deer and rabbits out of the garden, we spotted a badger sticking its

The half-mile Grand Allée of Castle Hill is lined with a precise planting of Norway spruce beside a long, wide stretch of lawn.

masked gray-and-white head out of its hole. Woodchucks (also known as groundhogs and marmots) and badgers dig burrows, are fierce fighters, and have keen appetites. But the brown woodchuck more often is found in forest-edge habitats devouring farmers' fields and gardens and putting on weight for winter. Badgers are flesh eaters, marauding other burrows and eating their unlucky inhabitants.

Inside the enclosure, walk to the middle of the wall on the right and pass through the gate. From outside the gate at 0.15 mile, you look down upon the roof of a private house. Turn immediately to the left, following post markers through the woods.

The climb is fairly steep, but the wood-chip path is well marked through a deciduous forest of mature white pine and shagbark and shellbark hickories. As you emerge from the woods, the sudden view of the Great House is quite a surprise.

Proceed left with a low retaining wall embellished with eagles and dolphins to your right. At 0.3 mile, you'll reach a parking lot (reserved for Great House functions). From the parking area, walk along the road, noting a round stone water reservoir on the left. At the main asphalt access loop, turn right and descend. The access road is one-way, and if you walk on the right you will see any traffic coming up Castle Hill.

At this juncture are several ornamental trees, including a wonderful large flowering dogwood. Continue a few yards and cross the road at 0.4 mile to see the remains of what once was an elaborate sunken rose garden designed by rosarian Harriet Foote (1863–1951). Two thousand roses were planted in four beds centered on a central bed, pool, and fountain, and encircled by a rose bower pergola supported by pillars. The Mediterranean-style garden hangs on the edge of the hill with an unobstructed view of the sea.

Opposite the rose garden and through a gate on your right are the formal Italian ornamental gardens, which provided floral arrangements for the Great House. On one end is a balcony overlooking a pool, and at the other end sits a pair of octagonal teahouses linked by a trellis. Continue a gradual descent on the access road through thickets of rhododendron and mountain laurel. Continue past the turnoff to Steep Hill Beach on the left. (This beach is beautiful but reserved for private functions; the day we were there, the rest rooms were closed.)

Remaining on the asphalt road, pass the beach parking area to the left, and you'll come to the 160-foot-wide and impressive

Grand Allée ("Mall"). To the left, this 0.5-mile allée extends to the ocean.

To return to the Great House, turn right on the Grand Allée and walk in the shade of the tall Norway spruces toward the Casino (Italian for "little house"). One house was used for billiards and also served as a ballroom. The little house on the opposite side of the mall doubled as bachelors' quarters and changing rooms for a saltwater swimming pool. The double staircases connecting the two buildings have been completely reconstructed. Turn left onto the road before the ballroom casino and circle around to the right on a gravel drive and path leading through a mature stand of maple trees to a set of wide wooden stairs. At the top of the stairs you will be on the left edge of the allée, with the Great House directly before you.

Walking to the left of the Great House, you come to a terrace and bench built into the wall, commanding excellent views of the ocean. Wind your way to the back of the house and the clearing where you first emerged from the woods. Retrace your steps back to the parking lot.

Hours, Fees, and Facilities
The Great House may be closed, but the trails are open from 9:00 A.M. to sunset. A fee of $5 per car is charged.

For More Information
The Crane Estate, 209 Argilla Road, Ipswich, MA 01938; 978-356-4351.

Pines Trail

Parker River National Wildlife Refuge at Plum Island (4,662 acres)

Newburyport, Massachusetts

Trip 6

Distance: **0.3 mile**
Type of walk: **Loop**
Approximate time: **15 minutes**
Difficulty: **Easy**

A spacious pitch pine grove on a knoll overlooking wetlands of the Parker River tidal estuary.

Getting There

From the Maritime Museum on Water Street in Newburyport, drive 3.2 miles south on Water Street (which turns into the Plum Island Turnpike). After crossing the bridge to Plum Island, take the first right onto Sunset Road, where a large sign directs you to the Parker River National Wildlife Refuge. Drive 0.6 mile to the entrance gatehouse, information center, and main parking lot. From here, drive 4.0 miles along Island Road to the Pines. Park directly in front of the trailhead.

Special Features

- Observation deck and benches
- Bird watchers' paradise
- Osprey nesting platform
- Trail accessible for people with disabilities

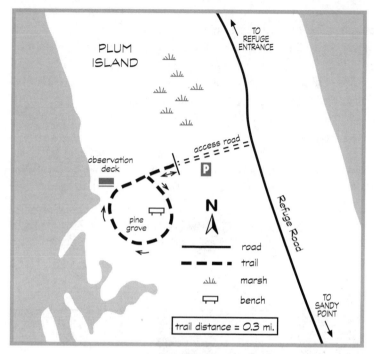

PLUM ISLAND

TO REFUGE ENTRANCE

access road

observation deck

P

N

pine grove

—————— road

– – – – trail

⊥∟ marsh

⊏⊐ bench

Refuge Road

TO SANDY POINT

trail distance = 0.3 mi.

Pines Trail

This is a wonderful, open location. Yellowlegs, sandpipers, Canada geese, and other water birds fly in and out of this tidal area. Most likely, you'll see bird watchers lined up with tripods and scopes along the edge of the parking lot overlooking the marsh. (Parking spaces can fill quickly.)

The Pines Trail begins at the parking lot. The 5-foot-wide trail with stone dust hardpack is well designed and universally accessible. Most of the walk is level, ascending and descending gradually only in a few spots around the entire loop.

If you have good binoculars, you'll likely spot yellowlegs here. Greater and lesser yellowlegs look similar except for their respective 14- and 10-inch lengths. Both have long needle-like bills characteristic of seashore water birds that poke their beaks into soft, water-filled sand for morsels to eat. The greater yellowlegs, with its gray-and-black-checkered back, is easier to identify. But this bird's trademark characteristic is the conspicuous yellow of its long legs.

From the parking lot, follow the hardpack pathway constructed by Youth Conservation Corps of Parker River National Wildlife Refuge in 1997 and 1998. In 40 yards, turn left at the junction.

In another 50 yards, the trail enters a small grove of pitch pines. These pines have 4-inch-long needles in groups of three; the bundles are called fascicles. Sea breezes whisper through the pines, and chickadees, pine siskins, and smaller birds take refuge on the branches. You can recognize the pine siskin, a fluttery finch, by its bold brown-and-white streaks from head to tail.

From an observation desk a short distance from this knoll, you can watch ospreys feed their young in large nests on high poles.

Continue along the trail up a slight grade through a stand of pines along the shore of Parker River Sound. The footpath curves around to the right. At the crest of the gentle rise is a spacious deck with built-in benches overlooking expansive wetlands. Although you can't see the Atlantic to the east, areas of low wetland grasses are visible, from Bill Forward Pond in the middle of the barrier island on your right to the fringes of Broad Sound at Parker River on your left. Plum Island Sound is fed by four rivers, including Parker River and Plum Island River (a runoff from the Merrimack River mouth), as well as Atlantic tides around the southern tip of this intriguing tidal barrier island. The sound forms a channel between the mainland and the island. Once we saw three ospreys nesting on top of a high platform on a pole, one of them in midmeal.

Ospreys circle above the water searching for prey. Then with tucked wings, they dive straight toward the water catching the fish in their talons and fly the catch back to their nest. Although their white underwings are seen mostly as ospreys fly overhead, these brown birds with long, narrow wings have white on their head, neck, and body. Osprey nests grow larger year by year because the ospreys return to old nests from season to season. This trail is short but a pivotal place for watching and listening to bird life and smelling the fragrant pines.

Hours, Fees, and Facilities
Parking fee of $5 per car.

For More Information
Parker River National Wildlife Refuge at Plum Island, 261 Northern Boulevard, Newburyport, MA 01950; Phone: 978-465-5753.

Hellcat Freshwater Marsh Trail

Trip 7

Parker River National Wildlife Refuge at Plum Island (4,662 acres)

Newburyport, Massachusetts

Distance: **0.7 mile**
Type of walk: **Loop**
Approximate time: **45 minutes**
Difficulty: **Moderate**

A boardwalk loop through a beach plum orchard and freshwater marsh on the Parker River, alive with migrating birds and waterfowl.

Getting There

From the Maritime Museum on Water Street in Newburyport, drive 3.2 miles south on Water Street (which turns into the Plum Island Turnpike). After crossing the bridge to Plum Island, take the first right onto Sunset Road, where a large sign directs you to the Parker River National Wildlife Refuge. Drive 0.6 mile to the entrance gatehouse, information center, and main parking lot. From here, drive 3.5 miles along Island Road to the Hellcat parking lot, area 4, located on the right.

Special Features

- Freshwater marsh
- Waterfowl observation blind
- Boardwalk and benches
- Beach plum blossoms in May
- Spring and fall warblers

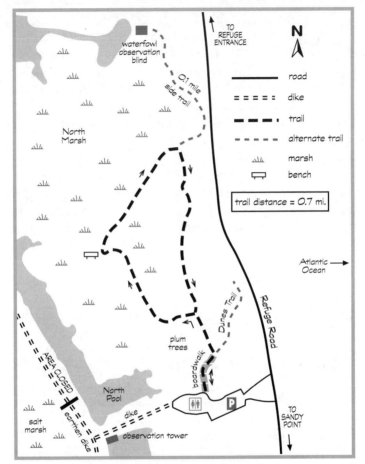

Hellcat Freshwater Marsh Trail

Plum Island Sound is fed by four rivers, including the Parker River and the Plum Island River (a runoff from the Merrimack River mouth), as well as Atlantic tides around the southern tip of this intriguing tidal barrier island.

The 4,662-acre Parker River National Wildlife Refuge—encompassing most of Plum Island and the Parker River estuary—was established in 1942 to protect critical nesting and feeding habitat for migrating birds. The refuge is accessible along the 6.3-mile Sunset Road, with numerous pull-offs, observation towers, platforms, and several trails. Bird watchers flock here in spring to observe the migrating warblers and some of the 300 other species sighted in the refuge. On one April day, we spotted ruby-crowned kinglets, hermit thrushes, and yellow-throated warblers.

The Atlantic beaches in the refuge are closed from April to August, when endangered piping plovers are nesting and raising their young. Open year-round, Sandy Point State Reservation, located on the southernmost tip of Plum Island at the end of Sunset Road, provides seaside access and views for picnicking, sunbathing, and recreation.

Deer roam the Parker River Wildlife Refuge, making this prime deer tick territory in warmer weather. For protection against deer ticks and Lyme disease, it's advisable to wear a hat, long-sleeved shirt, long pants tucked into socks, and shoes that cover your ankles and to stay on the boardwalks and pathways.

Friends of the Refuge hosts an annual Plover & Wildlife Festival in mid-May when the beach plums are in bloom. Children and adults can delight in the touch tank and tide pool walks, warbler banding demonstrations, and bus tours to locations usually closed to the public.

With its proximity to Newburyport and its diverse appeal, Plum Island and the refuge are apt to draw crowds of nature lovers. When this happens, Parker River Road is closed to ease the bumper-to-bumper traffic. One way to avoid the crowds is try to get there early on a weekday, if possible during the off-season.

At the Parker River Refuge, a boardwalk on the Hellcat Trail leads from wooded wetlands to the freshwater grasslands that are protected by an earthen dam.

Both the Hellcat Freshwater Marsh Trail and the Hellcat Dunes Trail (walk 8) begin at the boardwalk west of the Hellcat parking lot (area 4) near the rest rooms. Interpretive brochures are available here.

About 200 yards from the trailhead you reach a **Y** junction where the Dunes Trail branches off to the right. Continue on the Marsh Trail boardwalk, circling in a westerly direction through an orchard of wild beach plums *(Prunus maritima)*, native to the north Atlantic coast. The boardwalk provides an eye-level perspective on the 20-foot trees, dwarfed by Atlantic wind and weather. The white blossoms of this Plum Island namesake are profuse and splendid in May. During the spring, stagnant pools beneath the trees keep the moisture-loving plum trees well watered and provide vernal pools for deer and birds. The well-maintained boardwalk keeps your feet dry and also protects plants and insects of the understory.

At Stations 2 and 3, you'll see in the distance to the south an observation tower and a long earthen dike built in the 1940s. The dike impounds fresh water from the Parker River for migrating birds on the Atlantic flyway. Marsh grasses provide food for migrating waterfowl and help filter and purify the water.

If you're bird watching, Station 4 has a bench where you can rest and look for hooded mergansers, mallards, pintails, and other waterfowl in the common reeds and cattails. Several species of herons live in the refuge. You can recognize great and little blue herons by their long legs and S-shaped necks. The green heron is similar in size to the little blue but is chestnut colored with greenish yellow short legs. Black-crowned and yellow-crowned night herons hunch like bitterns in the reeds and grasses while they fish at dusk.

At 0.5 mile, you reach a T junction where a boardwalk side trail leads 0.1 mile north (left) to a waterfowl observation blind.

Returning to the junction with the main trail, continue straight, looping back along the Marsh Trail boardwalk through the bayberry shrubs and plum trees to the junction with the Dunes Trail. Turn right to return to the parking lot.

Hours, Fees, and Facilities

Parking fee of $5 per car.

For More Information

Parker River National Wildlife Refuge at Plum Island, 261 Northern Boulevard, Newburyport, MA 01950; Phone: 978-465-5753.

Hellcat Dunes Trail

Parker Island National Wildlife Refuge at Plum Island (4,662 acres)

Newburyport, Massachusetts

Trip 8

Distance: **0.6 mile**
Type of walk: **Loop**
Approximate time: **20 minutes**
Difficulty: **Moderate**

This boardwalk trail explores barrier island dunes in all stages, from secondary sand dunes sheltering shrubs and pines to primary (oceanfront) dunes with low-growing plant life.

Getting There

From the Maritime Museum on Water Street in Newburyport, drive 3.2 miles south on Water Street (which turns into the Plum Island Turnpike). After crossing the bridge to Plum Island, take the first right onto Sunset Road, where a large sign directs you to the Parker River National Wildlife Refuge. Drive 0.6 mile to the entrance gatehouse, information center, and main parking lot. From here, drive 3.5 miles along Island Road to the Hellcat parking lot, area 4, located on the right.

Special Features

- Elevated boardwalks
- Black pine and rare dune plants
- Elevated deck on three-story-high sand dunes overlooking the Atlantic

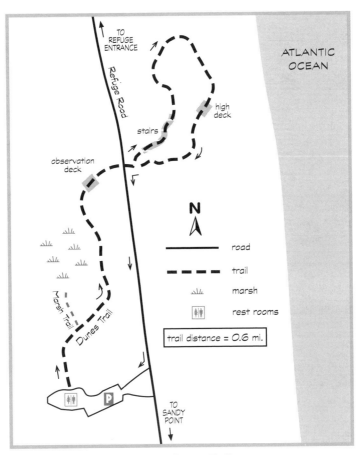

Hellcat Dunes Trail

The Hellcat Dunes Trail shares a trailhead with the Hellcat Freshwater Marsh Trail (see walk 7). Both trails begin at the boardwalk west of the Hellcat parking lot (area 4) near the rest rooms. Interpretive brochures are available here.

About 200 yards from the trailhead, bear right onto the Hellcat Dunes Trail boardwalk (the Freshwater Marsh Trail branches off to the left). When you're 175 yards past the trail junction (Station 2), you will see a healthy stand of black oak and pine in the lee of a high back-dune area. This is the widest part of Plum Island, and these high dunes run parallel to the ocean, offering a barrier against high winds and salt spray.

In another 100 yards, the boardwalk bridges a swamp in a stand of red maple at Station 3. Here the leaf buildup absorbs seasonal rainwater in the declivity between dunes, forming a micro-ecological zone of woodland species and plant life.

Climb the steps up to Refuge Road. Watch for bicycle and car traffic and cross with care.

The steps continue winding up a wooden scaffolding above a 50-foot dune (Station 4). This scaffolding protects the dune's flora and nesting seabirds from foot traffic. The tangle of thorny greenbrier seen here (also called catbrier) might well be the origin of the trails' *hellcat* moniker. Once caught in a nest of these briers, you'll find it hard to extricate yourself without getting scratched—another reason to stay on the designated boardwalk.

Continuing on the east side of Refuge Road, you'll be climbing secondary dunes before an overlook of the Atlantic Ocean's primary dunes—the coastal dunes fronting the ocean. Northeast winds wear channels through the primary dunes from sand deposited by the ocean. A breech in the primary dune channels funnels wind and sand through, forming secondary dunes behind the front lines.

Station 5 calls attention to hardy black cherry trees twisted and dwarfed by the relentless Atlantic winds. A carpet of beach heather *(Hudsonia tomentosa)* also grows in the secondary dune zone. The leaves of this false heather are covered with fine hairs to collect mist and reflect the sun's rays. Its interconnected root mat helps prevent erosion and provides nitrogen for other plants—thus stabilizing the secondary dune community.

Facing south at Station 6 you can see some of the Austrian black pines in the distance that were planted on the island to control erosion when the refuge was established. This hardy tree was selected because it thrives in poor soil and harsh environments. The dark silhouettes of the pines march over the seascape like tall evergreen sentinels.

Looking over the handrail of the boardwalk at Station 8, you'll see a tangled thicket of wild beach plums, which provide

A cantilevered boardwalk and platform near 50-foot-high sand dunes offers glimpses of the Atlantic.

food for birds, rodents, deer, and other species living on the island.

At 0.5 mile, a high platform (Station 9) overlooks the primary dunes and the wide blue Atlantic. These dunes are covered with beach grass. The genus name, *Ammophila*, literally means "lover of sand," and here it has a lot to love. Like beach heather, beach grass has an extensive root system of interconnecting rhizome runners that send up new shoots. Also like beach heather, the grass anchors the sand and provides a habitat for other plants to grow. While the rhizomes collect some water, the taproots extending more than 30 feet supply most of the water to the beach grasses. The blades of beach grass are slender so they don't dry out from the sun and often curl for protection from damaging winds.

From the deck, the boardwalk leading back to the road is a direct series of stairs. To return to the parking lot, you can either walk 0.1 mile along the road or backtrack through the woods past Stations 3, 2, and 1.

Hours, Fees, and Facilities
Parking fee of $5 per car.

For More Information
Parker River National Wildlife Refuge at Plum Island, 261 Northern Boulevard, Newburyport, MA 01950; 978-465-5753.

Eliza Little Walking Trail

Spencer-Peirce-Little Farm (230 acres)

Newbury, Massachusetts

Distance: **1.0 mile**
Type of walk: **Out-and-back**
Approximate time: **45 minutes**
Difficulty: **Easy**

A pastoral walk across old farmland from a seventeenth-century farmhouse to the Merrimack estuary.

Getting There

From I-95 (Exit 57) in Newburyport, take MA 113 east, which becomes MA 1A (High Road). Follow MA 1A for 3.7 miles through Newburyport, then turn left onto Little's Lane and drive 0.3 mile. Spencer-Peirce-Little Farm is on the left. Park at the visitor center.

Special Features

• Working farm since 1635
• Part of the Bay Circuit Walking Trail
• Historical farmhouse tours, educational programs, and gift shop

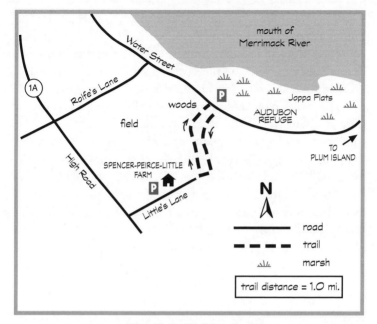

Eliza Little Walking Trail

The Eliza Little Walking Trail is part of the 170-mile Bay Circuit Walking Trail, which makes a half circle from Kingston Bay to Plum Island around greater Boston. The circuit, first proposed in 1929, now passes through fifty cities and towns, connecting more than seventy-nine protected sites such as this.

Driving down Little's Lane, the access road to the Spencer-Peirce-Little Farm is an impressive allée of ancient maple trees leading to the farmhouse that was lived in continuously from 1690 to 1986. The Littles, a tenant farm family, bought the property in 1861, and their descendants lived here until securing protection of the farmstead through the Society for the Preservation of New England Antiquities (SPNEA), which also conserves thirty-four other properties in the region. Taking a tour of the house and grounds gives a historical perspective, but you can walk around freely anytime from dawn to dusk.

The trail is named Eliza after the Littles' youngest daughter. Eliza never married and lived on the farm her whole life. The trail begins just beyond a giant copper beech to the right of the old brick facade of the farmhouse. An informational kiosk with maps and brochures stands at the edge of the farm field. Follow the mowed swath on the right edge of the expansive field. A few white-topped guideposts mark the trail as it follows the mowed swath on the right side.

Look for old apple trees on your right at about 200 yards. Apples are among the Rose family's 3,000 species of trees, shrubs, and fruit trees, including peaches, almonds, apricots, and plums; they all have five-petal blossoms. Colonial settlers brought the common native apple (*Malus pumila*) of southeastern Europe to the New World. Grafting of this apple produced many other varieties, including the Spitzenburg, a favorite of Thomas Jefferson.

At 0.1 mile, cross the dirt road to the farm field on the other side and spot a white-topped guidepost. Glance back at the farmhouse and imagine how difficult brick was to come by in precolonial America. Such a brick home was a sign of wealth and stability, unlike the plentiful wood and fieldstone houses. Imagine, too, views straight to the Merrimack basin near Plum Island. Wild grapevines entangle growth along the field periphery. Morning glory, beach rose, white and red clover, and sumac all grow within the first 0.3 mile on your immediate right. Wild carrot, also called Queen Anne's lace, with its white lacy flower

From the 1690 Spencer-Peirce-Little farmhouse, a trail leads over some of the oldest settled land in the country.

on top of frilly leaves, is especially fond of pastures and farmland.

The trail hugs an overgrown border with the farm field on the right. As always, avoid poison ivy, which favors woods edges and open roadsides. Remember the rhyme: "Leaves of three, let it be."

The trail curves left along the field. At the end of this short curved section, another white-topped guidepost marks the way.

At 0.42 mile, the trail begins to curve to the right along a shrubby border of wild carrot, morning glory, beach rose, and purple vetch. Then, in 100 yards or so, the trail narrows at a foliage arbor. Pass through this tunnel-like section, which opens onto a field. According to a local resident, the famous aviator Amelia Earhart (the first woman to fly solo across the Atlantic Ocean) once landed in this vacant field on the right.

Continue walking, now with shrubbery on your left, until you reach the two-lane Plum Island Turnpike (Water Street) at 0.5 mile. At this point if you wish, you can cross Plum Island Turnpike to the Joppa Flats Audubon Wildlife Refuge, an observation area on the estuarial basin between the mainland and Plum Island. Retrace your route to the farmhouse and trail-head.

Hours, Fees, and Facilities
There's no fee for walking.

For More Information
Spencer-Peirce-Little Farm, 5 Little's Lane, Newbury, MA 01951; 978-462-2634.

Drumlin Trail

Old Town Hill Reservation (495 acres)

Newbury, Massachusetts

Distance: **1.3 miles**
Type of walk: **Loop**
Approximate time: **45 minutes**
Difficulty: **Moderate**

*Expansive distant views of the Parker River estuary
from a 168-foot-high glacial drumlin used for three
centuries as a coastal landmark.*

Getting There

From Newbury Town Hall on MA 1A (High Road), drive 2.6 miles south to Newman Road. Turn right onto Newman Road and drive 1.0 mile to the Old Town Hill sign, where there is roadside parking.

Special Features

- Sweeping seacoast views from the partially cleared summit
- Rich variety of trees
- Fall hawk migration lookout

Old Town Hill is one of several noncontiguous sites making up the Bay Circuit Walking Trail, which starts at Plum Island and

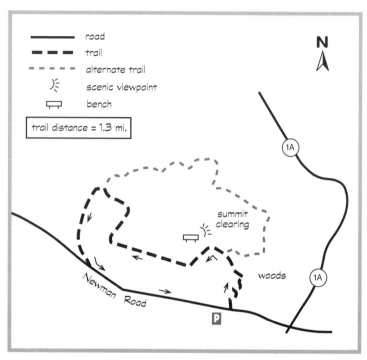

Drumlin Trail

ends in Duxbury south of Boston. This property is cared for by The Trustees of Reservations, founded in 1891—a conservation organization in Massachusetts.

The sign at Old Town Hill reads: "A landmark for mariners. A self-guided walk for the curious walker." Old Town Hill has been a landmark since 1635 when early settlers built a meetinghouse at its base. In 1639 they ordered "a way 4-feet broad from the green below to the top of Great Hill." Native Americans called the area *Quascacunquen* for the falls on nearby Little River and reportedly had a burial ground here.

The well-planned trailhead to Old Town Hill seems to beckon with its pass-through gate and information board, shaded by a pair of tall Norway spruce. Many of these non-native ornamental trees were planted by Newbury residents at the turn of the twentieth century.

Initially the trail follows switchbacks up the steep hill (168 feet at the summit). In effect you're climbing a drumlin, a mound of sediment dumped by the Wisconsin glacier many thousands of years ago. This is one of numerous drumlins in the vicinity of Boston, including the drowned cluster of drumlins that form the Boston Harbor Islands.

On the lower slopes you see the silvery trunks of Atlantic white cedar trees that have not weathered the harsh winter storms or foot traffic. Other trees on the base slope comprise a periphery forest of skinny aspen, pin cherry, and buckthorn shrubs. Pin cherry trees grow to about 30 feet, with leathery, shiny, oval leaves and black fruit eaten by a variety of birds. Like the plums that grow in this area, pin cherries are members of the Rose family.

At 0.2 mile, you reach a grassy clearing with benches on the summit. From this vantage, it's like looking at a topographical map. Humidity and a leaf canopy cut down on visibility in summer, but still, it's quite a view. In the coastal haze we could make out Hampton, New Hampshire, and the Seabrook power plant to the north, Plum Island and the Parker River estuary and marshlands (walks 6–8 below), and the outline of Castle Hill (walks 4 and 5) to the south.

Three rivers empty into the Atlantic Ocean near here—the Merrimack to the north, the 5-mile-long Little River at the base of the island, and the Parker River, flowing 15 miles from Boxford to the sea. Each day these rivers cleanse the Great Marsh—a collective term for these combined coastal estuaries. The Great Marsh encompasses 20 miles of coastline from Gloucester, Massachusetts, to Hampton, New Hampshire, and 25,000 acres of tidal estuary.

The open mowed meadow on top of the hill provides viewing of red-tailed and Cooper's hawk migrations in fall and warblers in spring. A stiff prevailing wind whistles through the tall Eastern white pines.

The entrance to Great Hill leads to the top of a 168-foot-high drumlin, an ice age sediment mound serving as a seacoast landmark since 1635.

After circling the clearing for the views, return and pick up the trail just to the left of the benches and head back into the woods. At 0.5 mile on the left are a few old apple trees, remnants of an orchard when much of this land was farmed. On the right is a high mowing that, again, looks out on the Atlantic.

Now begins the descent from the drumlin. Atlantic white cedars (identified by their silvery bark and gray-green flat frond branchlets) are much healthier and quite large in this area. At 0.7 mile, the path becomes gravel, and at 0.9 mile is a stand of tall red pines identified by their red bark.

At 1.0 mile, turn left onto Newman Road. Stay to the left of the road along the embankment of Old Town Hill. On the south side of the road is a vast area that has succumbed to bulldozer and building development. Walk back along the road 0.3 mile to what early settlers called "the lower green" at the trailhead.

Hours, Fees, and Facilities
Open daily, 8:00 A.M. to sunset. There is no fee.

For More Information
The Trustees of Reservations, 978-356-4351; www.thetrustees.org.

River and Pond Trail

Maudslay State Park
(480 acres)

Newburyport, Massachusetts

Distance: **1.6 miles**
Type of walk: **Loop**
Approximate time: **1¼ hours**
Difficulty: **Moderate**

Century-old paths on a former estate take in field, forest, the wide Merrimack River, and a secluded spring-fed pond.

Getting There

From I-95 (Exit 57), take MA 133 east for 0.5 mile. Turn left onto Noble Street immediately before St. Mary's Cemetery and drive 0.2 mile to a stop sign. Following signs to Maudslay State Park, turn left onto Ferry Road, drive 1.0 mile, then bear right onto Curzon Mill Road. Continue on Curzon Mill Road for 0.2 mile to reach the park entrance, with the headquarters on the right and parking on the left.

Special Features

- Magnificent century-old hardwood groves and white pines
- Spring-fed "Flowering Pond" with lush plantings
- Merrimack River views
- Handsome stone bridges

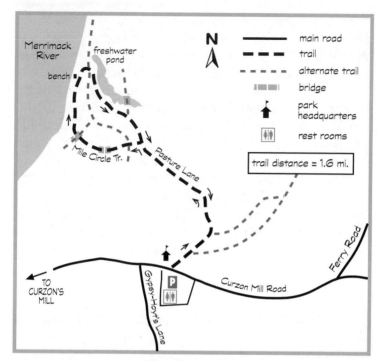

River & Pond Trail

Maudslay State Park offers you a look at a legacy from the past, with landscaping, forest plantings, paths, and old foundations dating back to the mid–nineteenth century.

This estate property along the south side of the Merrimack River was known as Laurel Grounds, for the profusion of small pink or white mountain laurel blossoms in May and June. The Moseley family settled here in 1805, and in the 1860s Edward Moseley bought many acres of the Laurel Grounds by the Merrimack River. Over subsequent decades, family members built substantial homes on the grounds overlooking the river. Moseley heirs also bought property, and the gardens became a meeting place for several notable writers, including Ralph Waldo Emerson and John Greenleaf Whittier. At one time in the late 1800s, Whittier (who wrote several poems about the Moseley estate), Emerson, John James Currier, and other celebrities attended parties and Shakespearean plays held on these grounds.

Helen Moseley kept a diary spanning thirty-four years of improvements to Swann Cottage (the main house, which became known as Maudesleigh, after the family's ancestral home in England) and the rest of the estate: stables, a tennis court, five stone bridges, the extensive Laurel Grounds, and several farms that had been acquired. Other improvements included greenhouses, a kitchen garden, a water reservoir, and the planting of 5,000 white pine, hemlock, ash, and elm trees.

Today the foundations and gardens are all that remain. The state of Massachusetts acquired the property in 1985 and developed it as a state park.

This is one of our favorite parks. In summer Maudslay's tall, stately trees offer a cool and shady sanctuary. The paths are well maintained, and the gardens are exquisite. Flowering plants in this park are many and varied—trilliums in April, dogwoods in May, azaleas in June, Indian pipes in July, and asters in August.

A multiuse park, Maudslay features many trails specifically designed and designated for walkers, bikers, or joggers. Narrow, bike-tire-wide paths parallel some wider walking paths so that bikers and hikers don't collide. The Merrimack River Trail has been kept rather wild and narrow, while the manicured garden paths such as the Mile Circle offer a more cultivated stroll.

To get to the trailhead for this walk from the parking lot, cross Curzon Mill Road and enter a pass-through gate in the stone wall along a large mowed field. In the first 10 yards you'll pass a few paths coming in from the right, but keep on the main trail, curving left onto Pasture Lane. A bike path parallels the lane. At a clump of pasture pines at 0.15 mile the descent is steep and gravelly, so watch your step.

Eastern white pines predominate on old estates such as this one, and so-called "pasture pines" often have three to six trunks. Farm animals, browsing among young white pine trees, would break the slender trunks, causing new trunks to form.

Continue through a stand of hardwoods. American ash can be too tall for a glimpse of the canopy but may be identified by its straight ash-gray trunk. Shagbark hickory is easy to recognize because of its bark, which appears to be shedding.

In an oak grove at 0.2 mile, look for black and pin oaks. Both have pointed leaves and gray furrowed bark, but the lobes of the pin oak leaf are deep and narrow, whereas the black oak leaves are broad like the predominant Northern red oak.

Rhododendron blossom in profusion along the banks of Flowering Pond on the old Maudslay Estate.

The great majority of trees on the estate are a century old, and in this section of the park many grow to 90 feet tall. At 0.3 mile, this combined River and Pond Trail levels off. At 0.4 mile, three trails converge. Take the wider trail to the left, which makes the 1.0-mile circle loop clockwise, joining the Merrimack River Trail along the river and then returning to this junction.

Gradually, the century-old path curves upward through the beech forest. Gray beech trunks are smooth, and the thin leaves of the airy canopy turn papery in fall. Helen Moseley's house wasn't far from here; her diary of 1907 reads: "Made paths through the 'Mile Circle'—extended the path from the lower garden to the beeches." The old Borderline Trail mentioned in the diary cuts in from the left and continues past two stone bridges, built by Helen in 1915. At the second and larger bridge, the trail bends to the right, passing a high rhododendron hedge on the left and an open area to the right.

At another mammoth pasture pine, veer right along the high escarpment of the river. At 0.7 mile, a bench overlooks a wide section of the Merrimack. This planned and planted forest is predominantly Eastern white pine, some more than 100 feet tall, and because their canopy is so high this section of the trail has a spatial grandeur. At the second bench a small path (part of the Merrimack River Trail) hugs the high river embankment. Views of the Merrimack from here are exhilarating. Curve around on the wider Mile Circle path. Now comes the crowning glory of this walk—the Flowering Pond. Fed by a nearby spring, the pond provides habitat for finches, catbirds, warblers, cardinals, and orioles. Rhododendron cascades down to the water's edge, and on the opposite shore a tangle of vines, wildflowers, honeysuckle, and ornamental plants proliferate.

The rhododendrons bloom into late June in a display of white blossoms with just a hint of blush.

Walk toward the picturesque arched stone bridge at the pond's inlet. When you reach the turnoff to the left that leads over the bridge, curve around to the right on the Mile Circle. Fine-needled hemlock branches droop gracefully over the path, and suddenly you realize you're back at the junction with Pasture Lane and have completed the Mile Circle. Bear left at the junction and return on Pasture Lane 0.3 mile back to the pass-through gate in the stone wall.

For More Information

Maudslay State Park, Curzon Mill Road, Newburyport, MA 01950; 978-465-7223.

Hedge Drive Trail

Maudslay State Park

(480 acres)

Newburyport, Massachusetts

Distance: **1.5 miles**
Type of walk: **Loop**
Approximate time: **45–60 minutes**
Difficulty: **Moderate**

A manicured nineteenth-century estate with raised-bed gardens, frontage on the Merrimack River, hedgerows, and arbors.

Getting There

From I-95 (Exit 57), take MA 133 east for 0.5 mile. Turn left onto Noble Street immediately before St. Mary's Cemetery and drive 0.2 mile to a stop sign. Following signs to Maudslay State Park, turn left onto Ferry Road, drive 1.0 mile, then bear right onto Curzon Mill Road. Continue on Curzon Mill Road for 0.2 mile to reach the park entrance, with the headquarters on the right and parking on the left.

Special Features

- Flowering rhododendrons, mountain laurels, and roses
- A white pine forest
- Wonderful views of the Merrimack River

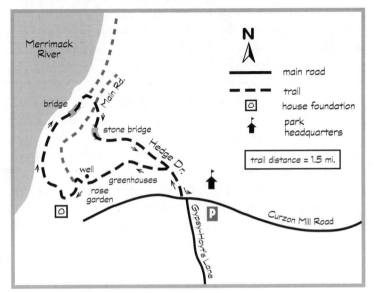

Hedge Drive Trail

The two Maudsley State Park walks in this book are clockwise loops around various parts of the former estate grounds and plantings, both joining up with the Merrimack River Trail for a stretch, then doubling back. On this walk, you see the formal Moseley Estate plantings.

The Hedge Drive Trail begins at a stone wall opening 100 yards west of the Maudslay State Park headquarters on Curzon Mill Road. The trail begins along Hedge Drive, skirting a softly rolling field on the right and bordered by stately, ancient maple trees on the left.

At the first **Y** junction (in about 300 yards), turn left (Hedge Drive continues straight) and pass through a grassy alcove lined with rhododendron and mountain laurel, two hardy evergreen shrubs. Mountain laurel (*Kalmia latifolia*) thrives from sea level to altitudes of 5,800 feet. Covered with pink or white blossoms in May and June, this shrub was the original namesake of the Moseley estate, formerly known as Laurel Grounds (see walk 11). Also growing here is Norway spruce, a non-native ornamental tree favored by many early-twentieth-century residents in this area. Norway spruce cones hang down from branches; their needles grow from nods, or small pegs, on twigs.

Turn left at the next **Y** junction, and at 0.3 mile enter the formal garden area, composed of greenhouse foundations (built circa 1900), a few intact cottages and maintenance buildings, and terraced flower beds. Follow the path through the walled garden—low brick walls topped with slabs of gray granite. Spruce hedges, high pines, and oaks surround daisies and pink and yellow roses on the periphery.

From the walled garden, the path leads through a maple and oak forest. At 0.46 mile, you pass by an old well encircled by granite and covered with a slanted wood roof. Follow the path for a few yards and turn left onto Main Road (no sign), which leads to a grassy field a few yards away. Turn right onto the faint path lined with huge oaks, which leads to the old foundations of the main house of the Moseley estate. The house was razed in 1955, leaving only the outline of the foundation. Straight ahead you can see the mighty Merrimack River flowing from its source in the White Mountains of New Hampshire, which once powered the booming textile mills in New Hampshire and Massachusetts during the nineteenth and early twentieth centuries.

Proceed across the open lawn around the foundation between two large oaks. Small signs on both oaks read

This old well on the Moseley Estate is surrounded by hardwoods planted in the 1890s.

Merrimack River Trail, which also winds through other sections of the park (see walk 11). Follow the narrow footpath, curving right, into the white pine forest, and walk with the river on your left. At 0.8 mile, descend through the woods (watch for roots and rocks underfoot), and in short order you pass between two giant white pines. Cross a small wooden bridge and walk through a rhododendron thicket, emerging at the foot of a cleared hillside. This spot commands a magnificent view of a broad bend in the Merrimack River.

Turn from the river and make your way up the grassy hill (there is no path here) a few yards to Main Road at 1.0 mile. Cross over a nicely constructed stone bridge (five stone bridges were built on the estate in 1915; walk 11 includes three of them). Head toward a junction a few yards away and walk left, ascending a snug, shady section of hemlocks and Eastern white pines—more than 5,000 white pines were planted on the grounds in 1904. Veer left as you approach a lawn enclosed by spruce hedges, saplings, and shrubs. A cultivated bed of roses and a grape arbor grow in the center of the enclosure.

Turn right down the high hedgerow and continue back to the trailhead.

For More Information
Maudslay State Park, Curzon Mill Road, Newburyport, MA 01950; 978-465-7223.

Ocean and River Trail

Salisbury Beach State Reservation (520 acres)

Salisbury, Massachusetts

Distance: 0.75 mile
Type of walk: **Loop**
Approximate time: **45 minutes**
Difficulty: **Moderate**

A family day-use and camping seaside area where the Merrimack River meets the Atlantic Ocean.

Getting There

At the junction of US 1 and NH 1A in Salisbury, take NH 1A north and drive 1.9 miles. At a large sign for the Salisbury Beach State Reservation, turn right onto State Beach Road and drive another 0.7 mile to the last parking area (Parking Lot 2) on the left.

Special Features

- Long, sandy beach and dunes
- Boulder jetty at the mouth of the Merrimack River
- Green crab fishing for kids
- Nature center, playground, and changing rooms

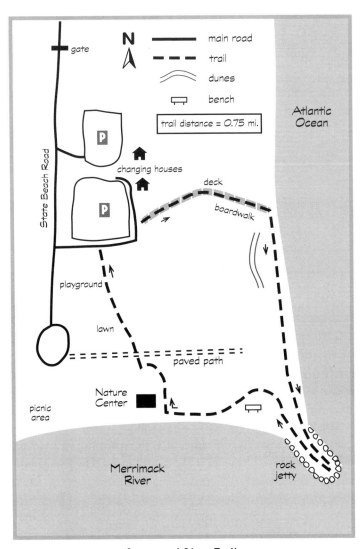

Ocean and River Trail

This is a first-class state beach with clean, airy rest rooms and changing facilities. It's a good idea to wear beach shoes with rubber soles because you'll be climbing a jetty and walking along a stone wall.

Begin the loop at the back of Parking Lot 2. A boardwalk is cantilevered over the golden sand dunes. The boardwalk protects the beach flora, which in turn retards sand dune erosion.

Dunes are formed when strong winds from the northeast blow inland (known as a nor'easter), sweeping sand into gentle slopes and valleys along the shore. The dunes create habitats for hardy tufts of common American beach grass, beach peas, and other low-growing plants that have adapted well to this shifting landscape. Some grasses have narrow leaf blades that funnel rain down to communal root systems; others send taproots several feet down to the freshwater aquifer.

As you walk across the dunes on the boardwalk, listen for the piping plover, a sand-colored seabird protected by its light plumage and saucerlike nests in the sand. It's also protected by humans working to bring back this endangered species. On many of these coastal walks, we heard its distinct high piping calls—a reassuring sign that protective efforts are succeeding. Another reason for boardwalks in this fragile environment is to protect nesting birds such as plovers.

Halfway across the boardwalk, a deck with a slat roof provides shade for sunbathers. From the deck comes your first wide view of the blue Atlantic. Once you're on the beach, turn right and walk toward the rock seawall at the mouth of the Merrimack River. Negotiating the beach is easier at the tide line where the sand is damp and compacted.

You'll probably see a number of blue mussel shells. Their abundance signifies more food for waders such as yellowlegs, white and blue herons, and the black-backed seagulls in this area. Mussels do well in colder waters and are being cultivated near the Isles of Shoals in New Hampshire.

As you near the seawall along the Merrimack River, note how the air temperature drops. The strong incoming tide brings noticeably cooler air from offshore.

Children like to clamber over the granite blocks of the seawall that begins on the beach. Farther out on the other end of the jetty, anglers cast into the river, mostly for striped bass. Be advised that the rocks of this breakwater are high and can be dangerous. Use caution if you decide to climb on them, and make sure to give fishers casting hooked lines a wide berth.

A lifeguard reportedly once saw bluefish "boiling" offshore and called bathers out of the water. Contrary to widespread belief, sharp-toothed bluefish don't attack swimmers, although they may bite people who happen to be very near bluefish during a feeding frenzy. Bluefish prey on other schools of smaller fish such as herring and immature fish, "chasing" them shoreward.

At the seawall (0.2 mile),

The small green crab has a body 3 inches long and is plentiful along the Salisbury breakwater at the mouth of the Merrimack River.

turn inland with the Merrimack River on your left. This river powered the nineteenth- and twentieth-century textile mills in Concord, Manchester, and Nashua, New Hampshire, as well as the colossal mills in Lawrence and Lowell, Massachusetts.

The area behind the seawall teems with green crabs, which children delight in catching in their pails. For closer inspection, they can gingerly hold the shell, keeping fingers well away from the pincers in front. Crabs have six legs (three on each side), plus a pair of pincers that allow them to tear apart mollusks, snails, worms, and other tasty intertidal tidbits. Crabs can be identified by size, color, and habitat. Large blue crabs and stone crabs are usually found farther south. Two common New England crabs are the smaller green crab (3-inch carapace, or body) and reddish rock crab (5 inches).

A bench is placed strategically overlooking the jetty just in front of the riverbank. Pass beyond it and climb up to a concrete seawall. The river is tidal here, and if the tide is up you can walk along this wall. Hold the hands of smaller children. At about 0.3 mile is a rock fishing pier. Sandpipers, nicknamed "peeps," peck at worms and fleas in the sand, and gulls walk the river mud flats as the tide washes fish and mollusks into the Merrimack basin. Ruddy turnstones, plump, russet-backed members of the Plover family, hop on bright orange legs and turn over pebbles and empty shells looking for their supper.

At 0.5 mile, you come to the nature center beneath a stand of Scotch pines. A naturalist is at the center from June through August and gives talks and shows films about marine ecology and the environment. The small facility also has a few exhibits.

You may continue strolling along the banks of the Merrimack about 0.5 mile around a crescent beach to a jut of land in the river. Otherwise, turn right at the nature center, walking past the John Bear Currier Recreation Center sign and across the lawn to a delightful beach playground with swings and a slide. Near the playground is a special crosswalk leading across the busy road and back to Parking Lot 2.

For More Information

Salisbury Beach State Reservation, Salisbury, MA 01952; 978-462-4481.

Hickory Trail

George Burrows Wildlife Sanctuary (31 acres)

South Hampton, New Hampshire

Distance: 1.25 miles
Type of walk: Out-and-back
Approximate time: 1 hour
Difficulty: Moderate

A beaver marsh and a mature deciduous forest with many shagbark hickory trees.

Getting There

From the junction of NH 150 and NH 107, drive south on NH 150 for 0.8 mile to Highland Road. Turn right and follow Highland Road for 0.8 mile to Woodman Road. Turn left onto Woodman Road and drive 0.4 mile to the sanctuary sign on the right. Park on the right-hand side of the road.

Special Features

- Roadside swamp
- Pleasant old town dirt road
- Shagbark hickories and other hardwoods
- Quiet butterfly and bird watching

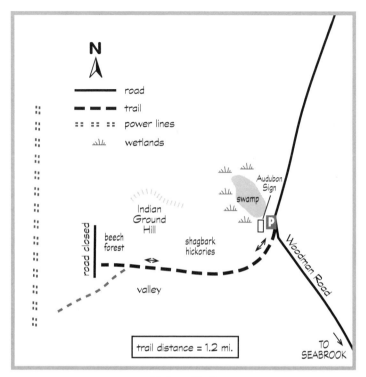

Hickory Trail

The sanctuary was named originally after George Burrows, former conservation chairman of the Audubon Society of New Hampshire, who purchased the land in 1965. An old dirt town road borders the southern end of the sanctuary. For the first 30 yards on the right, you see only a small section of the swamp, which extends into the sanctuary. Woodchucks, frogs, and woodpeckers are sighted here.

Walk up a gradual rise beyond the swamp past a tangle of water-loving grapevines. The New World was called Vinland by the Vikings for a good reason. In fall, purple and green grapes hang from the vines.

Low stone walls border the road on each side. In the nineteenth and early twentieth centuries throughout New England, walls for pastures, corrals, and boundaries were created from the stones cleared from the fields.

This walk can be an outdoor classroom for children. At 100 yards, the road curves through a hemlock grove on the right and a stand of red oaks on the left. Kids can identify a red oak tree by the reddish inner lines in the tree's trunk. To identify a hemlock, look up to see small cones hanging on the ends of its branches. Other trees, such as spruces, have cones that hang behind the tips of branches.

Shagbark hickory trees grow along many stretches of the trail, including a mature hickory to the right of the trailhead. Older shagbark hickories display an unmistakable "shaggy" bark that curls outward all around the tree trunk. Shagbark hickories are easy to identify in the leafless seasons. The trunks of relatively young shagbark hickories are smooth, but you can identify them by their leaves—five or seven toothed oval leaves, with the three largest leaves on the ends.

Shagbark hickory trees are prolific here, with purple-black hickory husks strewn over the ground in late summer and fall. Some of the husks are open for a view of the round nuts inside. Growing in the eastern third of the country, hickory trees produce a very hard wood used for tool handles and pilings, while green hickory has recently made inroads for barbecue-smoke flavoring.

Walking on a road in the woods is ideal for butterfly watching. Children can marvel at seeing these colorful creatures up close. Butterflies gravitate to borders of sunlight—an ideal place to look for the mourning cloak butterfly with gold color edging brown wings, the ubiquitous cabbage butterfly, and the large yellow-and-black swallowtail with "tails" extending from its back wings. Butterflies follow walkers awhile and then land on sun-warmed rocks or tall plants.

Continue on the dirt road, passing a faint side path on the left at 0.2 mile. After passing a pole gate on the right, look for an American beech grove. Beeches have smooth, muscular trunks and a papery thin leaf canopy.

This Audubon wetland is a good site for bird watchers.

A human presence in the woods creates a curiosity in certain wildlife, from butterflies to circling vultures. The first sign we saw of a turkey vulture was its shadow slipping across the road. The vulture, with a wingspan of an eagle, glided overhead low and slow for a look at us. Red-headed turkey vultures are carrion eaters and are constantly on the search for their prey. Friendlier black-capped chickadees (from the Titmouse family) follow walkers from tree to tree.

More hemlocks grow along the second half of the trail. At about 0.6 mile, the trail passes through terrain that pitches upward on the right to Indian Ground Hill (286-foot elevation) and on the left to Chair Hill (336-foot elevation). The road continues, angling through a shallow valley. A human-made roadblock of trees and brush is a good place to turn around; a wide footpath on the left through an opening in a stone wall leads down to a power line. Return to the trailhead via the same old town dirt road.

Ragged Neck Trail
Rye Harbor State Park
(63 acres)
Rye, New Hampshire

Distance: **0.5 mile**
Type of walk: **Loop**
Approximate time: **30–45 minutes**
Difficulty: **Easy**

*A park, granite seawall, and working harbor
with outstanding ocean views.*

Getting There

From NH 111 and NH 1-A in North Hampton, take 1-A north
for 3.9 miles to the Rye Harbor State Park on the right. Note:
The state park entrance is at a sharp curve 1.0 mile after the
marina entrance.

Special Features

- Exceptional seacoast views
- Marina jetty
- Isles of Shoals on horizon
- Harbor seal and cormorant watching

Starting at the park headquarters, an alleged bootlegger's
hideout during Prohibition, cross the parking lot to an unmowed

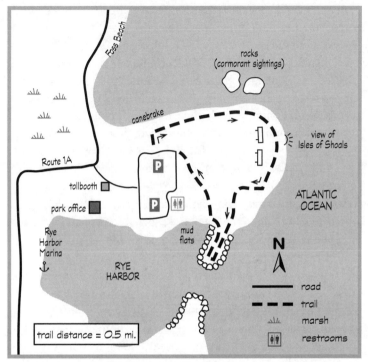

Ragged Neck Trail

area on the north side of the park. Turn seaward and walk the mowed lawn along a canebrake of feather grass. These feathery-tipped canes are 7 feet tall but can grow to 12 feet. On this exposed rocky peninsula, the little patch of feather grass provides protection for ducks and birds. In a few feet, wild raspberries and staghorn sumac offer vitamin-C-rich food for the song sparrow and catbird we heard calling from the dense undergrowth. The staghorn sumac forms a hedge of red conical berry bunches and fuzzy antlerlike branches from which it derives its name.

Hugging the sunlight on the periphery of the canebrake are stalks of salt-tolerant herbaceous seaside goldenrod. Its flat-topped flowers and leathery, gray-green leaves do not resemble the goldenrod with spraylike flowers found inland.

Walk around the picnic tables to the low granite wall that separates the mowed lawn from the rocky shore. Popping up here and there are daisies and beach roses on the high reaches of the rocky tidal shoreline. If you decide to walk among the rocks and explore the tide pools, wear rubber-soled shoes and stop before you get to the slippery yellow-green bladder wrack—a common rockweed that covers the intertidal area.

This side of the cove overlooks Rye Beach, where granite and a few quartz veins were deposited by a glacier thousands of years ago. New Hampshire is known as the Granite State and from its quarries come road curbs, bridges, and retaining walls, as well as the field granite of thousands of miles of stone walls.

Cormorants are often preening on the large, dark boulders near the entrance to Rye Harbor. This process stimulates the birds' oil pores, which in turn lubricates their feathers. Because of this oil coating on their feathers, cormorants can dive for fish without getting waterlogged. Nearly black-feathered cormorants have yellowish faces with brilliant red around their beaks and eyes. One evening we saw a cormorant on a flat table rock; the setting sun gave the diver the appearance of a firebird.

Continue to the rounded "head" above the "ragged neck." From the benches here on the point, it's as if you're sitting on the prow of a ship. Straight out to sea, the Isles of Shoals are prominent on the horizon about 5 miles distant. Combined with Portsmouth, this group of nine islands, discovered by Captain John Smith in 1623, comprised the largest inhabited area outside Boston during the seventeenth century. In this part of the New World, cod was king. At the Shoals in clear weather the ministers cut their sermons short for the codfishermen. Shoals dunfish, cod cured with seaweed on wooden fish flakes and exported to London and Spain, made many a fisherman wealthy. The population of the Shoals decreased in the eighteenth century largely due to overfishing, more lucrative endeavors on the mainland, and war. By the nineteenth century, the Shoals were again highly populated, this time with large 300-room resort hotels.

Huge granite blocks form a breakwater channel into Rye Harbor Marina.

On a clear day, you can identify the larger isles from the coast. North to south are Duck, Appledore (with the World War II radio tower), Malaga, Smuttynose (the site of several brutal axe murders in the nineteenth century), Cedar, Star Island with its white hotel (see walk 16), White Island and lighthouse, and Lunging (an early Londoners' trading post).

Continue around the periphery and soon you come to an unmowed meadow of red and white clover and goldenrod. Do not walk through it; poison ivy may be growing. Instead, find the cleared gravel path leading to the stone harbor breakwater.

Caution: If you wish to walk all the way to the end of the seawall, this part of the walk is difficult. Hold the hands of small children and go out only a little way onto the flat rocks. Older children and adults should wear rubber-soled shoes and premeditate every step. Although caution must be used when walking here, many anglers and sight-seers, including older children, enjoy clambering over the leviathan granite boulders.

The two sides of this seawall are like night and day. On one side are lobster fishers, whale-watching cruise ships, Isles of Shoals tour boats, and private sailing yachts. On the other, the deep blue Atlantic lilts or crashes against the breakwater. Jeffries Ledge, several miles offshore, serves as a feeding ground for 40-ton humpback whales, finback whales, the smaller minke whale, the endangered right whale, and harbor seals. Granite State Whale Watch is staffed by zoologists and biologists providing research information to the College of the Atlantic in Bar Harbor, Maine, and offers an opportunity for viewing sea mammals in their natural habitat. We have seen golden harbor seals swimming near here—so keep a lookout.

The harbor is full of sights and sounds. The last time we were on the jetty, we saw a beach-ball-size jellyfish floating in the blue-green water on the Atlantic side as a Shoals tour boat chugged in with crowded decks. One peculiar phenomenon of large expanses of water is that sound carries well. If someone is talking across the channel, you can hear every word clearly.

Returning to the first boulders on the jetty, make your way down the rock steps onto the pebble beach on your left. The tide usually leaves a patch of pebbles and mud to explore, which, upon closer inspection, reveals a prolific barnacle and periwinkle population. These toothlike projections of the barnacles on the rocks open when the tide comes in, and feathery tongues feed on minute particles of algae. Periwinkles are not native to New England but they thrive here; these small snails provide food for wading gulls and other water birds.

Head back toward the picnic pavilion in sight where the walk ends. As you return along the shoreline, tireless sandpipers may be nearby pecking at hoppers and other creatures on the sand. These small quick-stepping birds always seem a few steps ahead of you, as in Celia Thaxter's popular poem known by many New England schoolchildren:

> Across the narrow beach we flit,
> one little sandpiper and I,
> I watch him as he skims along
> uttering his sweet and mournful cry.

Hours, Fees, and Facilities
There is a $3 fee to walk the trail. No fee for children under 12.

For More Information
Rye Harbor State Park, Rye, NH 03870; 603-436-5294. www.nhparks.us

Star Island Shore Trail
Star Island (40 acres)

Isles of Shoals, New Hampshire and Maine

Trip 16

Distance: **1.75 miles**
Type of walk: **Loop**
Approximate time: **1 hour**
Difficulty: **Moderate**

One of nine islands 9 miles off Portsmouth, New Hampshire, with a wealth of migratory birds and seabirds, profuse wildflowers, an old-time hotel, and centuries of history.

Getting There

Exit 7E off I-95 turns onto Market Square. Parking for the ferry is at the Isles of Shoals Steamship Company dock in Portsmouth at 315 Market Street, across from the Sheraton Hotel. Be sure to call 603-431-5500 for the schedule of departures. Traditionally, the ferry departing at 10:55 A.M. lets passengers off at Star Island and then returns to the mainland at 3:45 P.M., giving visitors time to picnic, walk the Star Island Shore Trail, and relax on the island.

Special Features

• Guided ferry ride
• Historical monuments and a nineteenth-century hotel
• Shoreline exploration
• Marine lab touch pools and children's programs

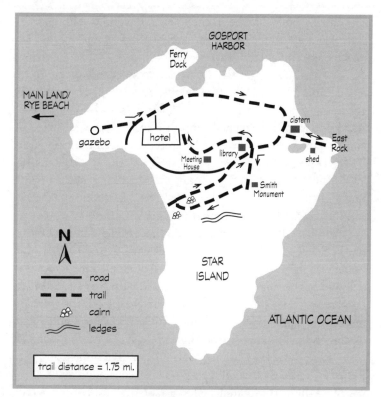

Star Island Shore Trail

The Star Island Oceanic Hotel has been a Unitarian summer conference center for more than a century. A conference may be in session while you are on the island, so keep to the hotel lobby and downstairs hotel rest rooms. Tap water is for washing only, but soft drinks and drinking water are available at the snack bar.

Day visitors are asked to abide by island rules: do not pick plants, and stick to the road and paths. Poison ivy is abundant, and nesting birds may be in the foliage. Beyond the hotel dock and playground area, children twelve years of age and under must be accompanied by an adult.

The path starts on the west end of the island at the Summer House, marking the site of the Star Island Fort built in 1653. The Sokokis and Micmacs in Maine and the Piscataquas and Pennacooks in New Hampshire were relatively friendly Native Americans. However, Boston regiments fighting King Philip (Metacomet) in Massachusetts marched north, taking land from Native Americans and settlers alike in the name of England. Skirmishes spread up the coast, and Fort Star's nine cannons announced occasional invasions.

All nine islands are visible from the Summer House. To the south, Seavey Island forms an isthmus with White Island—the home of a lighthouse. Seavey Island, like Appledore across the channel to the north, was overpopulated with herring gulls. At the end of the 1990s, an Audubon tern-protection project resorted to dogs and pyrotechnics to discourage the gulls, and by the end of the first season there were seven nesting pairs of terns. The terns now number several hundred and have been joined by roseate terns, plovers, and spotted sandpipers.

Walk from the Summer House past the Caswell Cemetery and turn left onto the road along the harbor. In the seventeenth century, the harbors were filled with fishing ships from England, and taverns, wharves, and crude stone houses strung up with hammocks for 600 to 800 fishermen littered the shoreline. Cod was caught, filleted, and cured with seaweed and sunlight on long wooden fish flakes. Called dunfish, this export commanded a high price from London to Spain. Lobster is the major catch these days.

Continue east along the Gosport Harbor (Shoaler for "God's Port") road as you walk toward the seawall, which connects Cedar Island to Star and Smuttynose Islands, forming a marina. The coastal flora includes beach roses, chokecherries, bull thistles, bright gold flat-topped tansy, and pale yellow wild mustard on slim 8- to 9-foot stems.

At 0.35 mile, hug the rocky shore of the harbor, walking up a hill toward the visible Tucke Monument. At 0.5 mile, turn left off the road onto a path beside a pond grown in with algae on the right; on the left is a stone-lined water reservoir with tannin-colored water. Follow the path to the left-hand side of a small barn. A few yards beyond the barn at a Y junction, veer right.

Notice the worn-down grass paths leading into the foliage. Muskrats that frequent the edges of the freshwater pools make these trails. Muskrats are aquatic with webbed toes and flat tails. They look like cat-size rats and live in water-bank burrows, conical habitats of grasses, and other vegetation. Muskrats eat roots and grasses, but occasionally they vary their diets with a frog or fish.

At 0.6 mile is a trap dike—what geologists call a deep channel in the granite—extending across the eastern ledges from the harbor to the ocean. When the tide comes in, the channel fills with water, except for a cave where one Betty Moody is said to have hidden during rumors of an Indian attack. While attempting to silence her baby's cries, the child was smothered. *Caution:* If you step into the dike at low tide and climb out onto Sunrise Point or East Rock, be careful; the surf comes up here, and the ledges are jagged.

Return on the path past the barn and two pools to the road and turn left. At 0.75 mile is the Vaughn Memorial Library, built in 1960, which contains a collection of hand-painted china and books by poet Celia Thaxter (1835–94). Celia grew up on White Island where her father, Thomas Laighton, was lighthouse keeper. Laighton purchased several islands and owned a boardinghouse on Haley's Island (Smuttynose). Celia married her tutor, Levi Thaxter, and while their parents were building a large resort hotel on Appledore, Levi became the minister on Star Island. One day, Levi's boat capsized; Levi survived, and soon thereafter Celia and baby Karl departed reluctantly with him for the mainland. Levi would never return to the Island. The library on Star Island is open to the public and well worth the visit.

Mainland garden clubs maintain Celia Thaxter's garden, located near the foundation of her cottage on Appledore Island. Thaxter established the first artists' colony in America at her cottage. It is here that celebrated guest Childe Hassam illustrated Thaxter's classic *An Island Garden* and taught her painting. Thaxter garden tours are very popular and must be arranged in advance.

Opposite the library is a turnstile from a bygone era when sheep and cows grazed the island. At 0.85 mile, if you wish to sit in the shade, a large cedar offers a pleasant canopy for several granite blocks below. Instead of walking the path to the Tucke Monument, turn left on a path next to the turnstile through a field of dense briers, roses, and bayberries. Bayberries grow directly from the stem. Settlers used them for making fragrant candle wax—and bayberry candles continue to be made today.

At 1.0 mile is a plaque on a pedestal to Captain John Smith, the first New Worlder to see the Isles of Shoals, in 1623; he later became governor of Virginia. Directly behind this monument, bleached ledges cascade down to what are called marine gardens. At low tide, you can examine starfish, seaweed, and other sea creatures in tide pools left by the surf. *Caution:* Make sure to wear rubber-soled shoes before venturing onto the ledges. If the tide and surf are up, stay back! In the nineteenth century, a certain Miss Underhill used to sit on these rocks. One day a wave crashed ashore and washed her away. The rocks are known now as Ms. Underhill's Chair in her memory.

Backtrack to the Smith Monument and walk the safe higher ledges toward a stone cairn at 1.25 miles, marking the southeastern point. Picturesque White Island lighthouse is in full view from these ledges.

Molten volcanic rock formed a mountain, which—during several million years and ice ages—was worn down to the base, leaving the Isles of Shoals. The general term for the rock is pegmatite, or an amalgam of granite in all its forms. White quartz and feldspar layers form veins in the rock, which is also embedded with fragments of tourmaline, small garnets, and silvery mica.

Turn around and backtrack a few yards until you see another large stone cairn on the left. It marks a path into the foliage northward to the Tucke Monument. Three kinds of roses—rugosa, Virginia, and polyantha—grow on Star Island and bloom throughout summer. Cross a small stone footbridge at 1.45 miles. In a few yards is the high granite obelisk honoring the Reverend Tucke, the minister on Star Island from 1731 until his death in 1773.

Black-back gulls are a familiar sight on Star Island.

A slab grave nearby marks the burial site of Josiah Stevens, who was sent as a minister to Shoalers and Native Americans in 1800.

Continue following the path north to the road, curving right in front of the Vaughn Memorial Library. Turn left at 1.5 miles onto a hilly path with the Parish House on your right. Climb the rocky hill toward the steepled Meeting House. The original was built on this site in 1685; the current building, built in 1800, has been restored several times.

Descend the 60-foot hill (the highest point on the island) via a gravel path leading to the hotel complex. The walk ends at the east end of the hotel porch, where you can sit on one of the rocking chairs and wait for the returning ferry. Another option is to walk down the lawn past the tennis courts to the Rutledge Marine Laboratory (afternoon hours are 1:00 P.M. to 4:00 P.M.). The lab is named after Lyman V. Rutledge, author of *Ten Miles Out: A Guidebook to the Shoals*, and boasts a 1,000-gallon saltwater tank with pollack, flounder, sea raven, and other Shoals fish. A smaller touch tank displays a variety of starfish, crabs, and smaller marine life. A naturalist is on duty, and the lab has a library of bird, plant, and other nature books.

Hours, Fees, and Facilities
There is a $23–$30 ferry fee depending on the length of your trip.

For More Information
The Star Island Corporation, 10 Vaughan Mall, Suite #8, Worth Plaza, Portsmouth, NH 03801; 603-431-5500; www.starisland.org.

Fuller Gardens Trail

Fuller Gardens
(2¹/₂ acres)

North Hampton, New Hampshire

Distance: **0.5 mile**
Type of walk: **Loop**
Approximate time: **1 hour**
Difficulty: **Easy**

*Expertly cultivated flower gardens with antique roses,
a Japanese garden koi pond, and a greenhouse
conservatory of exotic tropical plants.*

Getting There

From the junction of NH 1-A and NH 111, drive north on
1-A along the ocean for 0.1 mile. Turn left onto Willow
Avenue. Drive 0.1 mile and turn left into the large gravel parking lot at the Fuller Gardens sign.

Special Features

- All-American rose beds
- Japanese garden and koi pond
- Sunken garden beds and statuary
- Conservatory of exotic plants

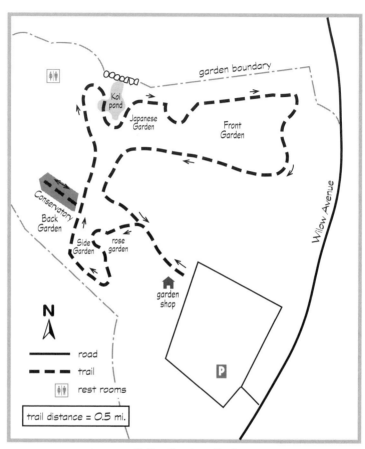

Fuller Gardens Trail

Fuller Garden was originally a cut flower garden for Viola and Alvan Fuller for their 1920s summer estate called Runnymede-by-the-Sea. Alvan Fuller was a successful automobile dealer who later turned to politics. He became a U.S. representative from

Massachusetts and later lieutenant governor and governor of Massachusetts. Runnymede-by-the-Sea has disappeared, but its exquisite gardens have thrived as a viewing garden since the 1930s. Today, a staff of professional gardeners cultivates and cares for 2,000 rosebushes in addition to a broad range of spectacular flowering plants grown for public enjoyment.

The trail entrance is to the right of the gift shop. On the left just inside the grounds is the Side Garden, with rose beds of every hue and variety and blooms for every season. Reproductions of Renaissance statuary and fountains add to the peace and beauty of the Side Garden. An apple espalier on the wood fence to the left was planted in 1935. An espalier is usually an apple or pear tree trained to grow flat against a wall or some other support as a sort of living bas-relief.

Near the espalier is Betty Boop, winner of the 1999 World Rose Award for All-American Rose. Like a wild rose, it is exquisitely simple—slightly cupped pale-yellow blooms with red-edged petals.

A pea-gravel path leads a short distance to the glass conservatory. This greenhouse protects tropical and desert plants from inclement New England weather. The enclosure features a fascinating array of plants, from the hefty, ball-like staghorn fern and the rare, delicate maidenhair fern to the vibrant passionflower, large fan palm, and ocotillo cactus.

When you exit the conservatory, walk through an arbor trellis a few steps and then turn left onto the driveway to the Japanese Garden lined with an arborvitae hedge. This garden provides a cool, tree-shaded enclave of flowering azaleas, a five-petaled Japanese maple, and a rock-sided koi pond—complete with a splashing waterfall and filled with gold, black, and silver

A Japanese garden and koi pond are part of the exquisite grounds at Fuller Gardens.

carp. A bench is available across a picturesque red bridge that arches over the pond.

Follow the sign that says Roses, Perennials to the raised landscaped terrace with statuary and descend the steps into the sunken Front Garden. Take some time walking along the northern side, lined with tall, blue delphiniums silhouetted against a dark green hedge bordering the garden. More roses grow here, including diminutive pink-on-white tea roses.

The maze of crisscross paths and head-high hedges form an intriguing labyrinth, which culminates in a central star. Turn slowly to the four directions for four different views of the hedgerows. At the far eastern end is the lovely original wooden garden gate set between the hedges.

Continue back on the southern side of the Front Garden to the Exit sign in the Japanese Garden and cross the driveway to return to the gift shop entrance. This ends the walk inside the gardens. But at the edge of the parking lot and to the south of the gift shop, take a look at the attractive Hosta Garden donated by the New England Hosta Society. Hostas are perennial plants originally from China and Japan that have been hybridized into a variety of hues, from green-blue to gold. These sturdy shade-loving plants have showy leaves that vary from broad to narrow.

In the far left corner across from the Hosta Garden stands an attractive linden tree, commonly called American basswood. Its rounded, tooth-edged leaf has a characteristic off-center heart shape at the stem. Standing center stage in the parking lot is a pin oak. The five-lobed leaves are so deeply cut into the overall shape of each leaf that the tree produces a lacy and delicate look, which, in turn, reflects the exquisite charm of Fuller Gardens.

Hours, Fees, and Facilities

Open daily 10:00 A.M. to 6:00 P.M., from May to mid-October. Adults $6; seniors $5; students $4. Children under 2, $2; groups over 10 people pay $4.50 each.

For More Information

Fuller Gardens, 10 Willow Avenue, North Hampton, NH 03862; 603-964-5414; www.fullergardens.org.

Odiorne Point Trail

Odiorne Point State Park (137 acres)

Rye, New Hampshire

Distance: 1.25 miles
Type of walk: Loop
Approximate time: 30–45 minutes
Difficulty: Easy

A history-laden walk through seven habitats alongside the picturesque Gulf of Maine.

Getting There

From US 1 in North Hampton, New Hampshire, take NH 111 east to NH 1-A, which runs along the coast. Turn left onto NH 1-A and drive north along the coastline for 8.0 miles. The entrance to Odiorne Point State Park is on the right and leads to a large parking lot.

Special Features

- Seacoast Science Center exhibits and indoor tide pool
- Picturesque Portsmouth-area shoreline
- World War II bunkers

The Seacoast Science Center building is an updated extension of the original stone 1923 Sugen House. During World War II

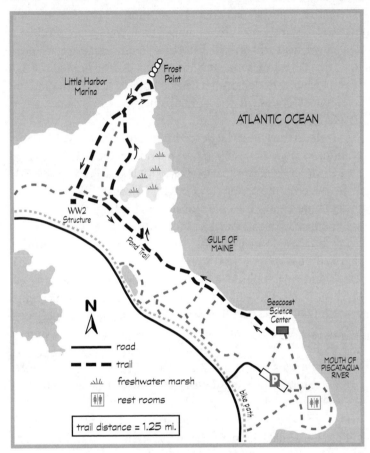

Odiorne Point Trail

the house served as officers' quarters; in the 1960s it became the park manager's residence. The complex you see today has several exhibit halls. Sugen Galleries describe 350 years of Odiorne people and life. American Indians called this land Panaway—

where the water spreads out. In addition to exhibits on salt marshes and meadows are a number of display tanks. Children can crawl beneath one tank for a different perspective, peer into a 1,000-gallon tank with important marine animals of the Gulf of Maine, or delight in the tide pool tank. Information on seasonal programs on the grounds and in the lecture hall is posted at the entrance.

Walk to the left of the Seacoast Science Center; behind the building is a small rotary for staff and handicapped parking. About 50 yards beyond the rotary is Odiorne Point trailhead. Walk beneath the canopy of a staghorn sumac; in 80 yards the rocky shore comes into view on the right, bright with tansies and goldenrod in summer.

Follow the footpath along the coast. Intermittently on the right, short side paths lead to beach beds of kelp and other sea wrack and tide pools. Low tide is a good time to examine sea urchins, limpets, eel-like gunnel fish, starfish, and other salt-water inhabitants. Tide-line deposits include black matchbook-size, hollow skate egg cases, pieces of washed-up finger sponges, and shells left by whelks, blue mussels, and moon snails.

As you walk along, imagine ancient cedar forests that once extended from Odiorne 9 miles to the Isles of Shoals. The last ice age dramatically transformed the landscape. As the ice sheet melted and slid over the land, it left a jumbled beach scape of sedimentary glacial quartz, sandstone, shale, and lime rock scraped from the land and redeposited here.

Two trails come in from the left at 80 yards and 160 yards but continue straight to see a panoramic view of the Gulf of Maine and Whaleback Lighthouse to the right.

At 0.3 mile, turn right at the Y junction located under mature maples. Perhaps a sleek otter will undulate across the trail in plain view—though faster than a speeding camera. Dark brown Canadian otters grow to $3^1/_2$ feet in length. They are supreme swimmers, designed with efficient ears and noses—both of which close underwater. With thick fur and fat, they are the graceful aquatic members of the Marten family.

Grapevines covering chokecherry trees and alder indicate a source of fresh water nearby. To the left at 0.45 mile a gaping concrete tunnel leads to the Seaman Battery bunker—a World War II defense for the Portsmouth Naval Shipyard. These long concrete casements are so well camouflaged with earth and brush that, from a short distance, they look like coastal hills blending into the tangled vines and prickly burdock (of the Aster family). Walk to the right of the bunker through a tentlike canopy of staghorn sumac. At 0.6 mile, on the left another part of the bunker looms out of the jungle of foliage.

Continue to the right of the bunker for a short distance to a T junction and turn right. In a few yards, turn right at the Y junction. This leads to a short loop around Frost Point. The peninsula looks over Little Harbor and a rock jetty. A prominent blue spruce grows on the point; nearby is a grand view of the Wentworth Marina. On Sandy Beach on the west of the peninsula, clam worms grow to 3 feet in length, living in burrows and emerging at night to prey on shellfish.

Giovanni Verrazano identified Frost Point in 1524. In 1759, the first settlers built a farm called the Pannaway Plantation. In the mid–nineteenth century, resort-era farming and fishing succumbed to Victorian vacationing and the Sagamore House Inn. During World War II this strategic point was turned into Fort Dearborn bunkers and headquarters.

Bear right at the next Y junction. At 0.8 mile, the loop ends; continue walking straight. Wild bright yellow tansy,

Low tide makes an excellent time to examine the rocky shore.

trailing groundnut, Queen Anne's lace, purple vetch, and other meadow flowers are prolific at this site. So are rabbits, which are seen frequently near their burrows in clearings among the tall grasses at Odiorne.

At 0.9 mile on the left is the other side of the battery bunker, overgrown like an ancient Mayan temple. Two other bunker tunnel entrances appear on the left in a few more yards. At 1.0 mile is a four-way trail junction. Turn left. In a few yards, partially hidden on the right, is a small bunkerlike structure. Shortly after, the path is lined with maples. These stately sap maples line an old carriage road in testimony to the manorial estates that once dominated the point.

The wide, smooth path leads straight back another 0.25 mile to the trailhead. We often pack a picnic lunch when we visit Odiorne Point State Park. The Atlantic salt air whets the appetite, and picnic tables are spaced alongside the ocean for spectacular views.

Hours, Fees, and Facilities

There is a $3 fee to enter the trail. No fee for children under the age of 12.

For More Information

Odiorne Point State Park, 570 Ocean Boulevard, Rye, NH 03870; 603-436-8043; www.seacenter.org.

Brooks Trail
Urban Forestry Center
(170 acres)
Portsmouth, New Hampshire

Distance: **2.0 miles**
Type of walk: **Loop**
Approximate time: **1 hour**
Difficulty: **Moderate**

A winding passage through roomy forest to the sparkling saltwater marshes of Sagamore Creek.

Getting There

From I-95 in Portsmouth, take Exit 3 onto NH 101. Turn right onto Elwyn Road. Continue on Elwyn Road across US 1 for 0.25 mile. The Urban Forestry Center is on the left and well marked. Take the access road to the parking lot, near the building complex and herb garden.

Special Features

- Demonstration gardens
- Sagamore Creek
- Vital salt marshes
- Water bird observation area

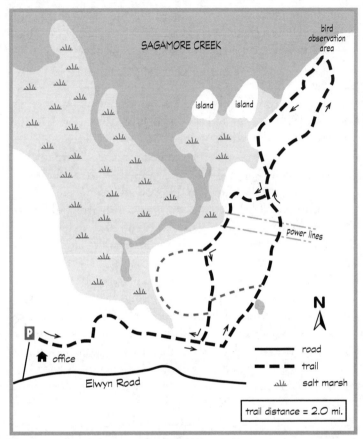

Brooks Trail

John Elwyn Stone (1922–74), a direct descendant of a 1650 settler, was an enthusiastic steward of land and sea and donated his estate for public inspiration and enjoyment. He preserved this tract against the encroachment of city expansion and commercial development. Managed by the New Hampshire Division of Forests and Lands, the Urban Forestry Center offers this woods walk to Sagamore Creek and provides a learning center for forest care, demonstrations, and many other programs.

John Elwyn Stone's estate provides technical guidance on the care of urban trees and shrubs, helping town conservation commissions and land developers with public urban forestry and other related projects. Programs for the general public include seminars about shrubs and trees that attract backyard birds, field trips, slide shows, and historical programs.

The Brooks Trail starts at the kiosk near the parking lot beside the office complex. Walk around an open field to a sign identifying Brooks Trail at the right corner of the large clearing (the tree identification trail is also in this area). Follow the white blazes of Brooks Trail, turning to the right after a few yards. Sagamore Creek salt marsh is visible through the forest.

Along this forested section for 100 yards are deciduous hardwoods—shagbark hickory, white oak, and American beech with its distinctive oval leaves that remain attached during winter. The black birch on your right shows how wide and inclusive the Birch family is, ranging in color from snow white to golden to black. All birches, including this black one, show characteristic "Morse code" dots and dashes on the bark. Black birch (also known as sweet, or cherry, birch) was the source for old-time birch beer, made from its sap in spring.

On the left as you walk the first 0.3-mile section is a 60-acre saltwater marsh. Sagamore Creek feeds this salt marsh, an ecologically valuable buffer zone between land and sea. It is one of four prominent rivers—the Spruce and Chauncey Creeks in Maine and the Seavey and Sagamore Creeks in New Hampshire—that converge at the mouth of the Piscataqua River in Portsmouth. These creeks mix fresh water with ocean salt water, thus producing an exceptionally vital system of plants, animals, fowl, and fish. For instance, crossing a small drainage ditch, 6- to 7-inch black snapping turtles may be seen in the backwater on the right.

At the first trail junction (a trail enters on the left), climb a slope, passing many deep green Solomon's seals. In spring, in moist woods as these, Solomon's seal produces greenish yellow blooms scarcely longer than 1/2 inch. The tubular flowers hang downward in pairs, a characteristic that is helpful in identification. Most likely you'll see the common 4-inch-long mud turtle. However, you might be fortunate enough to see the rarer yellow-green Blanding's turtle; it has been seen in the Portsmouth Great Bog, which was recently acquired by the Seacoast Land Trust.

The trail connects with a dirt road. Turn left and walk down this shaded road for a few minutes. At 0.5 mile, turn left to reach a compact, marshy pond on the right, somewhat hidden by roadside brush. This is the kind of primordial pool that supports life in all sizes and forms—frogs, dragonflies, kingfishers, and turtles.

Continue down the weedy road past beech and birch saplings. The bright white birches in the forest have two common names, stemming from practicality. Native Americans made canoes from white birch, hence the name *canoe birch*. Early settlers used white birch bark to write messages on, thus the name *paper birch*. The white bark is easily cut from the trunk, is thin like paper, may be shaped, and is waterproof. (*Caution:* Cutting into the bark damages healthy trees.)

A curious mix of sounds and sights reminds you that this indeed is an urban walk, even though the trail winds through a forest. In the distance, bell buoys ring, church bells chime, train whistles blow, and, up ahead, the path crosses under a power line. At the same time are heard the territorial *whirring* of red-winged blackbirds and the throaty croaking of frogs.

Veer right and pass two other trails entering on the left. These are open, gracious woods, but eventually the trail narrows and the foliage tightens to a single-file path. This signals that a point-of-land approaches where the trail loops around the rocky shoreline of Sagamore Creek.

At 1.0 mile is a designated water bird observation area for the great blue heron, northern harrier (hawk), glossy ibis with

Two trails diverge in the woods and both eventually come to Sagamore Creek and the salt marsh.

its long, curved, gray-black bill, and snowy egret with its black bill. Below the rocks, shallow sea-green water waxes and wanes with the tide. Across Sagamore Creek, forest and rocks line the banks.

On the right, salt marsh grasses extend to US 1 and a distant steeple. For centuries the wetlands, particularly the marsh grasses, were extremely useful for humans. These grasses were cut and dried on wooden poles, or staddles, for hay. Gradually, nature is reclaiming the nineteenth-century salt hay drainage ditches and channels. The grasses in the salt marsh are variations of basic spartina. Tall, frilly-topped cordgrasses grow immediately above the high-tide line; shorter marsh hay grows higher up on the mud flats.

Walk around the point and keep an eye out for the main trail. Before crossing back under the power line, look for an arrow blaze. Follow this trail to the right; it leads to a pine-needle path through white pines and other conifers. A narrow branch of a tidal inlet is soon reached where the salt marsh appears at nearly eye level. Once back in the woods, follow an arrow to a junction. A little beyond a footbridge, look for animal tracks in the mud. We saw otter and raccoon tracks well preserved in the wet soil. The five pads of the otter separate from the sole, whereas the raccoon's tracks look more like small human hands.

Keep to the right and return to the first section of the trail, about a five-minute walk. Turn right and retrace your steps another 0.25 mile to the trailhead.

For More Information

Urban Forestry Center, 45 Elwyn Road, Portsmouth, NH 03801; 603-431-6774.

River and Bridge Trail

Prescott Park
and Memorial Bridge

Portsmouth, New Hampshire

Distance: **0.6 mile**
Type of walk: **Out-and-back**
Approximate time: **I hour**
Difficulty: **Easy**

An urban walk through the gardens of Prescott Park along the busy Piscataqua River, and a walk on Memorial Bridge for a gull's-eye view of the historical town, tugs, tankers, and lobster boats.

Getting There

From I-95, take Exit 7 (east) onto Market Street. Drive south on Market Street from North Church in Market Square, downtown Portsmouth. At the first traffic signal, turn left onto Fleet Street. At the next signal, turn left onto State Street. Drive 0.2 mile on State Street and turn right onto Marcy Street (just before Memorial Bridge). Pass Strawbery Banke Museum on the right and turn right onto Hancock Street, following signs to the Strawbery Banke parking lot (on the right).

Special Features

- Prescott Park and seasonal gardens
- Piscataqua gundalow (a native river barge)
- Boat drawbridge and high river views

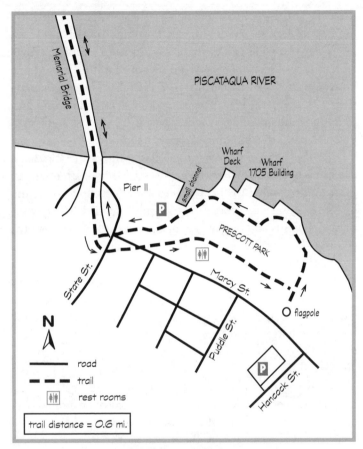

PISCATAQUA RIVER

Memorial Bridge

Wharf Deck

Wharf 1705 Building

Pier II

small channel

PRESCOTT PARK

State St.

Marcy St.

O flagpole

Puddle St.

N

road
trail
rest rooms

Hancock St.

trail distance = 0.6 mi.

River and Bridge Trail

Start at the flagpole across Marcy Street (opposite the Strawbery Banke parking lot). In January 1766, nine years prior to the American Revolution, the people of Portsmouth were the first to raise the colonial "No Stamp" (no British taxes) flag at this site. The flagpole commemorates this rebellion against paying British duty on goods entering Portsmouth Harbor.

Walk the wide garden path toward the Piscataqua River, which serves as a border between New Hampshire and Maine. Turn left and head toward Memorial Bridge arching over the river. On this paved river promenade, a shingle building built in 1705 stands over the water. During the festive summer at Prescott Park, this building serves as an art gallery.

To the left on Marcy Street are shingle and clapboard dwellings of the early fishermen who settled here after Captain John Smith landed in the 1620s looking for sassafras. He and his crew found strawberries instead and dubbed it Strawbery Banke. Taverns and marmalade madams soon flourished in this colorful "Puddledock Pub" area.

With the Piscataqua tidal river on the right, pass through the gate in a chain-link fence to an open area with new wharf boardwalks. In summer at the wharf, an authentic long Portsmouth river barge called a gundalow may be boarded for viewing. These barges plied the Piscataqua River from the 1600s to the 1930s, transporting everything from beer and fish to gunpowder.

At 0.15 mile, a superb granite whale statue basks in the open to the right, a tribute to the great migratory mammals that often are sighted off the Isles of Shoals and feed offshore at the continental shelf at Jeffrey Bank. Along the fishing wharves, the common bladder wrack bobs and sways in the lilting waves. Air bladders help buoy these weeds up when the tide comes in.

At the parking lot with a narrow channel lined with pines, turn left and walk out the park entrance, crossing Marcy and State Streets. Climb the steps to the bridge. Memorial Bridge was built in honor of the sailors and soldiers who participated in World War I. During World War II, nets were strung across the mouth of the wide river to keep enemy submarines from the Portsmouth Naval Shipyard. At 0.25 mile, pedestrian board-walks line both sides of the bridge alongside the Piscataqua River. The bridge may be drawn for the passage of a huge tanker, requiring a bit of a wait. To the right, the outgoing tide can carry a fishing dory swiftly past Great Island, Whaleback Lighthouse, and Odiorne Point for the 9 miles out to the Isles of Shoals. To the left, the incoming tide can carry a sailboat 15 miles inland to Great Bay. The Piscataqua is a powerful and important river.

At the end of the bridge, return on the other side. The traffic can be heavy, so use the crosswalk and make sure to hold

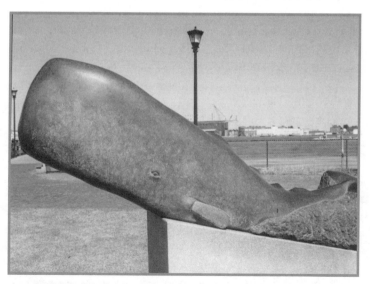

A granite whale basks in the afternoon sun, much like those sighted off the Isles of Shoals.

a child's hand. On the Maine side of the river west of the bridge, look for lobster traps and pots of metal or wood and lobster boats tied up at the wharves. Lobster restaurants are just across the bridge; the business in Maine and New Hampshire is highly territorial. Fortunately, cooler northern waters are ideal for these crustaceans. In winter, they migrate to deeper waters and hibernate on the bottom. Some of them winter in Great Bay.

Retrace your steps to Marcy and State Streets and reenter Prescott Park, returning on the path that leads past the concession stand and rest room facility (seasonal). Continue 30 yards to a brick path leading to a sunken garden, which is surrounded by a white picket fence and bordered by a rhododendron hedge. Seasonal flower beds are planted around three fountains, and crab apple trees provide shade. A short distance from this garden is a park road. Turn right and come to Marcy Street across from the Strawbery Banke Museum adjacent to the parking lot.

For More Information
Prescott Park, Portsmouth, NH 03801; 603-436-1552.

Oaklands Tunnel Trail

Oaklands Town Forest (307 acres)

Exeter, New Hampshire

Trip 21

Distance: **2.0 miles**
Type of walk: **Out-and-back**
Approximate time: **1 hour**
Difficulty: **Moderate**

*A popular multiuse trail in a mixed woodland near
a large tunnel under NH 101.*

Getting There

From NH 101, take Exit 9, 10, or 11 to Exeter. Beginning at
the central bandstand in downtown Exeter, drive 0.2 mile
north on Water Street. Turn right, through granite pillars onto
Swazey Parkway and drive 0.4 mile. Turn right onto Newfield
Road (NH 85). Drive 1.2 miles on Newfield Road, going under
railroad tracks over NH 101. Park at the entrance to Oaklands
Town Forest on the left.

Special Features

- Multiuse wilderness area
- Unusual pedestrian tunnel
- Glacial boulders

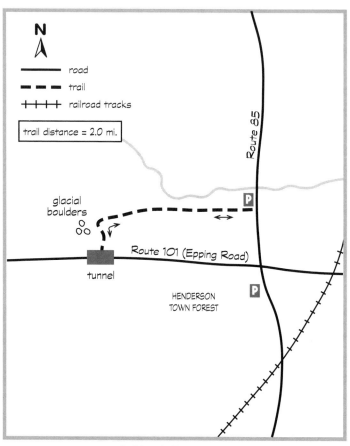

Oaklands Tunnel Trail

The trailhead at the parking area slants down a wide pathway through mixed hardwoods and conifers for 175 yards. In summer this section is grown in with raspberry and blueberry bushes. Cross a small stream and ascend an easy grade.

Caution: The Oaklands Tunnel Trail is popular with mountain bikers as well as walkers. Keep alert for mountain bikers, especially those approaching from behind. They usually warn of their approach with "Behind you," or something similar. Ascend a slight upgrade and a meadow appears 400 yards into the walk. Many field daisies and black-eyed Susans spark up the grasses during June and July. The familiar black-eyed Susan, a member of the Coneflower family, is known also as yellow daisy. The dark yellow flower perches on a single stem; its long petals droop slightly downward.

Reenter the woods and in another 100 yards pass through a thorny brier of red raspberries. Watch out for their thorny stems, called canes. A member of the Rose family, raspberries—lumped together with dewberries, blackberries, loganberries,

Metamorphic glacial erratic layered with a vein of quartz in Oaklands Town Forest.

and boysenberries—are called brambles. These prickly shrubs with edible fruits emerge full-blown every two years (the canes are biennial, the root system perennial). A single wild berry goes a long way in terms of flavor. Remember to use caution when tasting any wild edibles, and leave plenty for others.

At 0.3 mile, a stone wall appears on the right, and then you pass an array of glacial erratics. During the mid-1800s Louis Agassiz of Harvard University propounded his theory that ice age glaciers carried huge stones from the north. Then when glaciers melted and receded, they dumped boulders in these new locations, resulting in glacial erratics. Boulders of widely varying sizes and tonnage throughout New England are concrete examples of this theory. The Oaklands Town Forest area is full of them, including Fort Rock, found on a dirt road in the adjoining Henderson-Swazey Town Forest. At 0.5 mile at a T junction, turn left onto a blue-blazed trail. Enter the woods with more impressive glacial erratics on the right.

In another 0.1 mile, the trail descends the hillside. Here, traffic noise from NH 101 increases as you near the busy highway. Use the flat log footbridge over a short muddy stretch. Several yards later, at 0.72 mile, the fieldstone-faced tunnel beneath NH 101 comes in view. The trail leads straight through this arched, dark tunnel, with asphalt underfoot and streams of cars and trucks overhead. The entrance is protected on both sides by a chain-link fence. Kids will love it.

Emerge from the tunnel into woods again. A red-blazed trail takes over here, but this marks the end of this short walk. Retrace your steps to the parking area.

Swamscott River Walk

Swazey Parkway

Exeter, New Hampshire

Distance: 1.3 miles
Type of walk: Loop
Approximate time: 45 minutes
Difficulty: Easy

A pleasant town promenade along the
Swamscott River that flows to Great Bay.

Getting There

From NH 101, take Exit 9, 10, or 11 to downtown Exeter. From the central bandstand, drive north 0.2 mile. Look for granite posts at the entrance to Swazey Parkway on your right, and across from the American Independence Museum. You can leave your vehicle on the parkway itself or on Water Street. There is a parking lot at the public boat launch just before and adjacent to Swazey Parkway.

Special Features

- Wide Swamscott River views
- Urban promenade and benches
- Ornamental trees
- Historic gunpowder storehouse
- Universal access

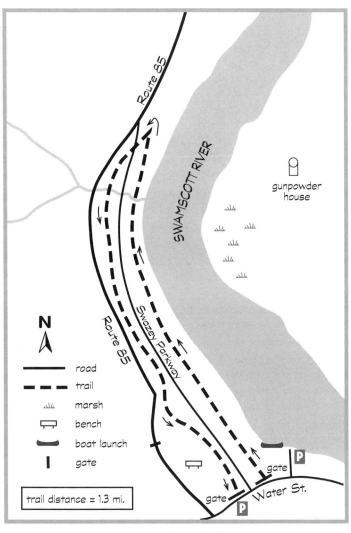

Swamscott River Walk

Exeter was one of the earliest precolonial settlements. To get here from the coast required sailing the tide up the Piscataqua River, crossing Great Bay, and sailing inland on the Swamscott River.

The trailhead is a sidewalk starting at the granite posts marking this lovely parkway, the gift of an eminent Exeter son, Dr. Ambrose Swazey, in 1931. This walk has sweeping views of the river, and the sidewalk extends along the riverbank with lawn and mature ornamental plantings on both sides of the park road. After entering the park, you'll see a tidal boat launch on the right for kayaks, canoes, sculls, and other boats. On the other side of a protective fence grow beach roses and a tangle of colorful wildflowers.

At one time this area was part of a dump, but in 1929 Dr. Swazey and others started acquiring land rights to create a beautiful approach to Exeter. Two years later he gave the parkway to the town. For the architectural landscaping they contracted the Olmsted Brothers, founded by Frederick Law Olmsted, designer of Central Park in New York City and the Emerald Necklace network of parks around Boston.

At 0.25 mile a sign states, Old Powder House Built in 1771, referring to a small brick building near the treeline on the opposite bank of the river. At 0.3 mile, full crowns of an old maple and white birch shade the promenade in summer. Native Americans in this area, most of them Piscataquas and Pennacooks who came from the north during summer, used white birch bark for the outer skin of canoes because it was waterproof and cut easily in broad strips. Birch wood, however, is soft and the trees rot easily, so a canoe frame was formed of hardwood such as ash splints.

Benches on Swazey Parkway provide a view of historic Exeter, including a brick powder house used during the Revolutionary War.

To the left of the park road is a platform stage for special outdoor events. During summer Swazey Parkway is closed to traffic one day a week for a farmers' market. At 0.4 mile, a rather ornate concrete deck extends over the river. A signboard indicates the gunpowder storehouse across the river. Powder captured from the British in New Castle on the Piscataqua River was stored here and later used in the Battle of Bunker Hill. Gunpowder also was stored here during the War of 1812.

A walking path across the river parallels this sidewalk. Dogs are not allowed on the Swazey Parkway grounds; you'll glimpse dog walkers on the opposite shore, which is clogged with pesky, invasive purple loosestrife, horsetails, and reeds.

Past the jutting dock, a sturdy stone wall retains river water. At 0.7 mile, two more stone pillars mark the end of the thruway from Water Street to NH 99. Turn around and, at 0.8 mile, cross the road to a beautifully landscaped small brook, which flows under the road into the river. We saw a large snapping turtle near this stream, and catbirds and robins swooped down to drink the fresh water.

Stay to the right of the road and walk the lawn—a great spot for picnicking. A sidewalk comes in at 1.1 miles. Benches are located near American holly, a prickly, leathery evergreen with bright red berries. In this area are an ornamental Norway spruce with upcurved branches and a majestic stand of short-needled, fragrant hemlock. The Swazey Parkway is a unique and delightful combination of a picnic area, river promenade, and thruway.

Heron Point Trail
Heron Point Sanctuary (32 ³/₄ acres)
Newmarket, New Hampshire

Trip 23

Distance: **0.7 mile**
Type of walk: **Loop**
Approximate time: **30–40 minutes**
Difficulty: **Easy**

A forested shoreline with a striking view of abandoned mill buildings, a waterfall, and a dam on the Lamprey River.

Getting There

In the center of Newmarket across from the public library on NH 108, drive 0.1 mile across the Lamprey River bridge to Bay Road. Turn right onto Bay Road and drive 0.3 mile to Meadow Drive (unmarked). Turn right onto Meadow Drive; the road passes through a trailer park. Drive 0.1 mile to the Heron Point Sanctuary access gate on the right. Turn right onto the narrow dirt access road and drive 0.3 mile to the parking area and information kiosk.

Special Features
- River shore and granite mill buildings
- Old-style fishing weir
- Dramatic split glacial boulder
- Extensive platform and boardwalk

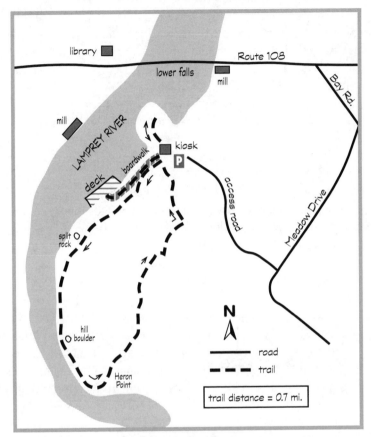

Heron Point Trail

Right away the Lamprey River, a major river that flows over falls through Newmarket into Great Bay, is visible through the open woods at the base of well-designed wooden stairs. The Lamprey is the only major river in New Hampshire that is contained entirely within state borders. The Swamscott Indians, a tribe of Algonquian-speaking Pennacooks of the north, settled here to fish and farm. Over the centuries, these falls provided power, bringing prosperity to the Newmarket shipping trade. The name of the river comes not from the lamprey eel but from John Lamprey, an early settler. Before Newmarket was incorporated as a town in 1737, the area was known as Lampreyville.

The trailhead is to the left of the kiosk as you face the river, but take a walk down the wooden stairs for a closer look across the Lamprey River. Gaze at the wide view of the town and its stalwart redbrick and gray granite mills. The falls that generate power to operate the mill are visible in the distance to the left of the huge mill building upriver.

Walk a little to the right onto the jut of land for a look at the dam. The view from the point offers an introduction to early New Hampshire integration of river power and mill town.

Return up the steps and enter the trail with the river on the right. In about 50 yards, veer right at the Y junction and onto the boardwalk. In a few more yards, at another Y junction (the trail returns to this point), descend a gradual flight of stairs to a deck platform overlooking the river. Built-in benches located here make this a restful place to observe mallards and other waterfowl such as herons.

Return to the junction and walk up a steep incline into the woods and away from the river (although the Lamprey River remains in sight for more than half this loop trail). As you ascend the hill, notice the erosion control on the right. Logs in a V formation on the downhill side retain soil from storm runoff. Without this control water runoff washes soil away from

Walking quietly on a trail can bring surprises around the next bend—like startling a great blue heron into the air.

roots, gouges gullies, and eradicates wildflowers and other woodland groundcover.

To the right sits a modest-size glacial erratic, a boulder transported by a glacial "conveyor belt" measuring a mile thick in this region. What is fascinating about this erratic is the dramatic split down the center, an example of the power of ice. When frozen water expands, and over the years the ice expand in the boulder's crevices, forcing the rock to crack. At 0.2 mile on top of the hill is another large glacial erratic on the right. Continue down the trail toward the Lamprey River and past a young shagbark hickory tree on the left. Native Americans boiled the nuts from shagback hickories to make a sweet hickory milk.

At the bottom of the hill, look across the river to the right to see a weir fish trap floating in the water. The trap is similar to those built by the Swamscotts to catch herring and alewives swimming upriver. The weir fish trap is fashioned of tall, thin tree branches woven together and lined up like a stockade toward the middle of the river. The tall branches of the trap catch fish that are blocked by the dam. The end of the weir works on the lobster trap principle—the fish cannot escape. This trap, labeled Chick's Weir, is touted as New Hampshire's only active weir.

The trail skirts Heron Point and then comes to a clearing. This is a pleasant spot to linger and watch the kayakers on the river.

At 0.35 mile, the trail turns to the left away from the river and up a slight incline past a grove of young cherry birch, gray birch, and red-osier shrubs. Red-osier dogwood has reddish twigs and commonly grows in moist locations. At 0.5 mile, turn left at a T junction (a faint trail leads to the right). Watch for a few staghorn sumacs, identified by their upright, hornlike cluster of fuzzy red fruit. The shrublike tree can grow to 20 and 30 feet; their branches exude a milky liquid when pressed and crushed. By the trailside in this moist area, we saw a large group of Indian pipes, the completely white "ghost flower" that has no chlorophyll and feeds on decayed organic matter in the soil.

At 0.55 mile, a T junction appears (the trail to the right loops back to the access road). Turn left and descend a gentle hillside until you see the Lamprey River and the trailhead.

Sandy Point Identification Trail

Great Bay National Estuarine Reserve (50 acres)

Greenland/Stratham, New Hampshire

Distance: 0.6 mile
Type of walk: Out-and-back
Approximate time: 30 minutes
Difficulty: Easy

Hands-on exhibits at the Discovery Center and a boardwalk exploration of Great Bay culminate with a visit to a woodland Native American camp.

Getting There

At the Stratham rotary junction of NH 108 and NH 33, turn east on NH 33 and drive 1.5 miles. Turn left onto Depot Road and drive 0.9 mile. At the stop sign, turn left onto Tidewater Road and drive another 0.2 mile into the Sandy Point Discovery Center parking area.

Special Features

- Touch-and-feel saltwater pool
- Old-time gundalow (river barge)
- Boardwalk and benches for watching birds and observing the bay

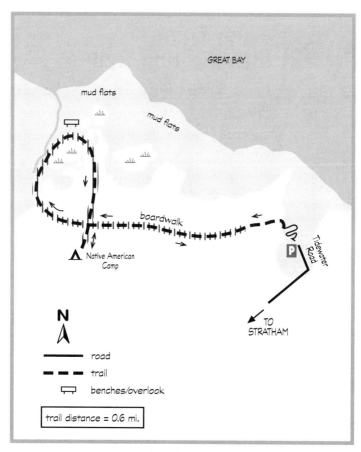

Sandy Point Identification Trail

Of all the twenty-five national estuarine research reserves in the United States, Great Bay is located farthest inland (15 miles). It's the largest reserve, comprised of nearly 4,500 tidewater acres, 48 miles of shoreline, and 800 coastal acres of protected salt marshes and woodland. Water ebbs and flows from this bay with daily tides. The Piscataqua River in Portsmouth is the conduit for the major tidal force, while the estuary receives fresh water and nutrients from the Swamscott, Lamprey, and Winnicut Rivers.

Before starting your walk, stop at the Discovery Center to learn about Great Bay through the many interesting exhibits. You are encouraged to dip your fingers into a saltwater pool and touch horseshoe crabs, flounder, eels, and other marine creatures found in Great Bay. Volunteers and naturalists are on hand to answer questions and talk about kayak tours, summer children's programs, and adult discussions. Some equipment is on display from the estuarine research vessel that regularly samples the bay water for oxygen, nitrogen, phosphorous, salinity, and bacterial levels.

After visiting the center, walk to the rear overlook and take the stairs down to the trailhead. The 90-foot gundalow on display here is native to Portsmouth and the Piscataqua River and was in use from the seventeenth through the nineteenth centuries. These flat river barges hauled cargoes of everything from brick and wood to barrels of beer, fish, and gunpowder. Edward Adams was captain of this gundalow, one of the last on Great Bay.

A helpful guide map available at the Discovery Center highlights many salient features of an estuary. The map identifies two indicator species in the wetland forest along the moist terrain of the bay shore—shagbark hickory and ironwood. An indicator species is a plant or animal that is found almost exclusively in one type of ecological zone. For example, shagbark hickory and ironwood favor the moist soil bordering swamps. Shagbark hickory grows tall and wide and is easily identified by the "shedding" look of its bark. Thin ironwood trunks also have a distinctive look—blue-gray bark that is muscular and smooth.

Soon a convenient boardwalk elevates you above the soggy forest groundcover. Notice the pronounced transition to smaller trees and low-shrub wetlands. Spicebush (with yellow spring flowers) and witch hazel (with yellow fall flowers) both like the moist soil.

Also in the forested wetland, shallow tree "root knees" provide little pillows of soil for club moss. This moss is a primeval, soft green New England plant that regenerates by spores instead of seeds.

At 0.2 mile, an information sign explains the term *point pollution*, a site-specific source of contamination that can be controlled—an oil spill or sewage leak. Nonpoint source pollution, such as erosion and the leaching of fertilizer into groundwater and streams, cannot be traced to a specific source. Early in the twentieth century, for example, Portsmouth was a large beer producer. By-products from the breweries and other industries were

A boardwalk loop introduces visitors to ecological features of Great Bay.

dumped into the Piscataqua River and carried into Great Bay. Thanks to environmentalists such as Rachel Carson, who helped increase our awareness, and subsequent progressive environmental policies, Great Bay is now cleaner than it has been for centuries and wildlife is returning.

Keep an eye open for ospreys during your walk. In recent years, ospreys have returned to the bay in spring to nest and raise their young. As they circle high on the thermals (updrafts), they resemble the bald eagle. They hover over the water flapping their strong wings and plunge feetfirst into the water for fish. The bald eagle can steal a fish catch from an osprey in flight, never the reverse.

Upland and wetland forest and scrub are followed by transitional marsh, where currents, tides, precipitation, streams, and runoff contribute to the mixing of fresh and salt water. Now the boardwalk edges a peninsula that once was an island. Small-leaf cattail and spike grass are at the higher level of the marsh. Cattails and grasses break down at the strand line, where winter ice forms around their stalks, causing detritus—a fancy term for rotting piles of twigs and leaves. Slowly the detritus builds up, creating nutrient-rich soil where tree saplings grow. Eventually soil bridges can transform islands into mainland.

At 0.3 mile are benches for bird watching and gazing at the bay. Shortly beyond the benches is another sign illustrating high-marsh habitat where sticklebacks, silversides, mummichogs, and other fish live in the spartina grass. Low-marsh indicators are peat and sturdy cordgrass. The mud flats provide an oozy habitat for worms, clams, and mud snails.

At 0.35 mile, look for spindly black gum trees among an island jungle of tangled greenbrier, winterberry holly, and sweet pepper vines with heart-shaped leaves. Red-tailed hawks sit on the black gum branches while raccoons, otters, and muskrats tunnel through the undergrowth to dine at the mud flats. Their menu includes green crabs, mud snails, soft-shell clams, and an occasional newborn horseshoe crab.

At 0.4 mile is a large expanse of phragmites (pronounced *frag-mighties*), commonly known as feather grass. This is an invasive species, similar to purple loosestrife. It once formed a soil berm that blocked the water channel and displaced more advantageous plants in the marsh. Hundreds of volunteers had to clear more than 1,000 feet of feather grass in order to restore the water flows to the area.

At the end of the boardwalk loop section is the Woods Walk sign. Take the dirt path a few yards into the woods until you reach a woodland Native American camp with tree branch frames for shelters. Known generally as the Abenaki, eastern coastal Native Americans paddled these rivers in birch-bark and dugout canoes. In summer, some tribes migrated north to Lakes Pennacook, Winnepesaukee, and others, then rode the Piscataqua River to Great Bay in late fall to winter on the coast. Depending on the season, frames such as these were covered with animal skins or bark. Return the same way to the Discovery Center by way of the boardwalk.

Hours, Fees, and Facilities
The Sandy Point Discovery Center is open Wednesday through Sunday from 10:00 A.M. to 4:00 P.M., May 1 through October l, and weekends only in October.

For More Information
Great Bay National Estuarine Reserve, Depot Road, Stratham, NH; 603-778-0015.

Adams Point Trail

Great Bay National Estuarine Research Reserve (800 acres)

Trip 25

Durham, New Hampshire

Distance: **1.0 mile**
Type of walk: **Loop**
Approximate time: **1 hour**
Difficulty: **Moderate**

An extensive shoreline stretch along a scenic promontory of the Great Bay tidal basin.

Getting There

From the center of Durham, travel south on NH 108 for 0.4 mile; at the Y junction, turn onto Durham Point Road. Drive 3.6 miles on Durham Point Road to an access road. Turn left and drive 1.2 miles on the access road to the end. Toward the end of the access road is a state boat launch on the left, which is open to the public. Park in the spaces on the right. The Jackson Estuarine Research Laboratory at Adams Point is located to the left.

Special Features

- Views of Great Bay
- Tidal flats
- Bird watching from the cliffs

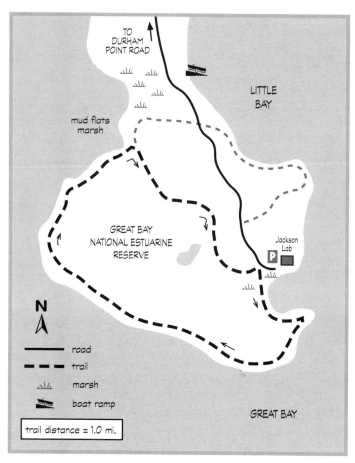

TO DURHAM POINT ROAD

LITTLE BAY

mud flats marsh

GREAT BAY NATIONAL ESTUARINE RESERVE

Jackson Lab

P

N

road
trail
marsh
boat ramp

trail distance = 1.0 mi.

GREAT BAY

Adams Point Trail

This inspiring walk skirts the edge of a section of Great Bay that has a 50-mile hidden tidal coastline. Much awaits the walker here—a sea cliff, forests, a field, and lingering shades of a bygone era. The shimmer of light on the water and flux of the tides in constant motion contribute to the grandeur of the expansive views of islands and inlets along the walk.

Two trails start at the parking area. The newer walkway, the Evelyn Brown Trail, begins to the left of an observation deck and takes a more inland route. The Adams Point Trail follows long stretches of the peninsula's shoreline. Enter the Adams Point Trail a few yards to the left of the parking area at the kiosk. Two large posts to the right of the access road identify the trailhead. A footpath to the shoreline leads to an overgrown field.

Cross the overgrown field, which is covered with sumac and a fair amount of poison ivy. *Caution:* The path also is lined with sumac, poison ivy, and thorny barberry shrub. Turn right when you reach the cliff with Great Bay ahead. The trail is clear and broad here, with the overgrown field to the right. The two Footman Islands lie just offshore. As you walk the ridge of the cliff, a few side trails lead onto the rocky shore. The rock ledges are covered with slippery knotted sea wrack. The "knots" are air-filled sacs that keep the rockweed afloat, allowing photosynthesis to take place. Eastern slipper shells (snails) and other organisms are exposed at low tide.

Great Bay is an inland estuary, covering 4,471 acres of open salt water, inlets, marshes, and mud flats. Near Portsmouth the Piscataqua River feeds into Little Bay, which in turn ebbs and flows into Great Bay, providing a variety of salt marsh and tidal creek wildlife environments. Adams Point forms part of Furber Strait—the opening where Little Bay to the north changes to Great Bay in the south. The jut of land now known as Adams Point was once used as a Native American camp.

Walk along the shoreline beneath a canopy of red oaks, shagbark hickory (with rough, peeling bark), and basswood—a broad tree with deeply furrowed bark and large, off-center, heart-shaped leaves. Pass through an opening in a stone wall. This land once was a working farm; look for traces of an old hayrack used for hauling hay and other farming equipment, cellar holes, estate roads, and stone pasture walls.

The Jackson Estuarine Research Laboratory comes into view. In the 1800s, this was the site of the "Reformation" John Adams home, where 1,500 people once came to hear him preach. The University of New Hampshire has operated the lab since 1970 to study the estuary and to locate sources of pollution so that Great Bay can avoid environmental degradation. Great Bay National Estuarine Research Reserve is managed by the New Hampshire Fish and Game Department and is under the guidance of the National Oceanic and Atmospheric Administration.

Ascend a steep shale embankment through wind-stunted beech, taller hemlock, and red pine. For a while the trail follows the ridgeline of a 100-foot bluff above the rocky, gray shale beach. Rock ledges jut out and form ideal balconies for scenic views of the islands and distant shores. Here the point curves. Continue through a stand of white birch and along the far side of the promontory above a marshy area. Gulls and great blue herons may be seen coasting the currents or pecking in the long, ribbonlike spartina grass and tidal flats for shellfish. Ospreys and bald eagles also have been seen flying over the sheltered bay.

The trail descends through a stand of white birch to the water. White birch bark was used by Abenaki Indians for canoes because this outer bark is light and waterproof. Walk along the plank bridge over a muddy backwater. Turn right at the junction immediately after the bridge and loop back uphill

A family enjoys the coastal scenery of Great Bay at Adams Point.

through the woods. At 0.5 mile, two tree trunks block the path. Notice as you climb over them the perfectly round holes drilled by members of the Woodpecker family, from the large pileated woodpecker to the smaller yellow-bellied sapsuckers, searching for insects burrowed in the rotted wood.

On the right side of the trail is a stone wall; on the left, a paved access road. Continue on the trail, pass an abandoned rusty hayrack on the right, and then cross through an opening in the stone wall. This spot commands some interesting sights. Directly across the field, a white obelisk burial monument of the Reformation John Adams family pokes above the weeds. The obelisk was erected in 1854 and is made of Durham granite and Italian marble. Twenty-four members of the Adams family have been buried in the vault. *Caution:* Poison ivy is prevalent near the grave site; investigate the grave from afar.

Just to the left behind the stone wall, an ancient, rotund hickory still bears nuts and provides shade for passersby. Turn left and skirt the wall, keeping the meadow to the right. A chiseled granite foundation on the right endures beneath the spreading taproots of a sumac grove.

You'll get a glimpse of a marina prior to reentering the parking area past the maple tree at the gate.

Hours, Fees, and Facilities
Information is available at the kiosk. Rest rooms are available.

For More Information
Great Bay National Estuarine Research Reserve, 225 Main Street, Durham, NH 03824; 603-868-1095.

Chesley Grove Trail

Wagon Hill Farm
(140 acres)

Durham, New Hampshire

Distance: **1.2 miles**
Type of walk: **Loop**
Approximate time: **1 hour**
Difficulty: **Easy**

*Rolling meadows and woodlands with shoreline
views of Little Bay and Oyster River.*

Getting There

At the intersection of NH 108 and US 4 in Durham, drive east
on US 4 for 1.9 miles. Turn right at the Wagon Hill Farm sign
and drive for 0.1 mile on the access road to the upper-level visitor parking.

Special Features

- Multiuse recreation on an 1804 farm estate
- Mix of lush meadows, shore, and woodland
- Picnic area and views of Oyster River and Little Bay

Wagon Hill Farm has been long identified by the old wooden
buckboard wagon on a hilltop silhouetted against the sky—the

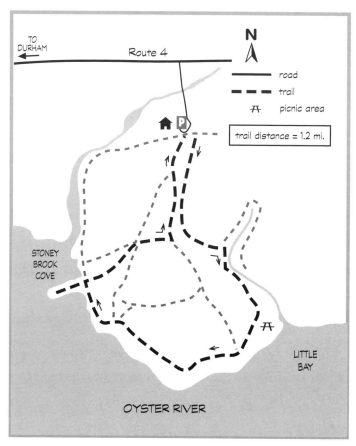

Chesley Grove Trail

scene of a thousand photos. The 1804 white clapboard farmhouse adjacent to the parking lot was the home of a family that planted and harvested the land for four generations, until 1960. The 100-acre tidewater farmland (another 40 acres of the property lies on the other side of US 4) was farmed for three centuries. In 1989 the town of Durham bought the property to preserve the open scenic vistas and provide an attractive year-round recreational environment for the local residents and the general public.

The trailhead is next to the upper parking lot and parallel to the old wagon, overlooking the trail side of the hill. Follow the wide, mowed, grassy path to the left downward through the meadow.

In the distance, Little Bay receives Atlantic Ocean tidal water from the Piscataqua River, which then flows into Great Bay. To the north, Oyster River winds through Durham. Walk through the meadow in late summer to encounter many monarch butterflies on migration south to avoid the colder northern temperatures of fall and winter. The meadow has many milkweed plants where monarchs hatch and grow, feeding on the plant's cardiac glycosides. The substance permeates the monarch's body and wings and is extremely bitter to its predators such as birds and snakes. If birds or other predators eat a monarch, they go into convulsions. As a result, birds stay away from monarch butterflies.

Smaller plants abound in the meadow, including the charming buttercup with its tiny, bright yellow blossom of five petals conspicuous above seven to nine ragged leaves. Hop clover has a yellow ball-like flower; its three-pronged leaf resembles the Irish shamrock. Low-lying meadow plants such as vetch and purple and white field vines also grow here. Birdsongs from catbird, meadowlark, and song sparrow abound, especially in early morning.

This trail forms part of a 1.0-mile running loop. At the bottom of the meadow, about 300 yards into the walk, turn right at a **Y** junction. Skirt an overgrown, swampy area to the left, mixed with conifers, small willows, white Atlantic cedar with silver-blue berries, and scrub brush. Cross a ditch with a large white pine on the left and continue walking along a narrow dirt path for a short distance (less than 0.1 mile) through the woods.

At 0.5 mile is a large, secluded mowed lawn with picnic tables scattered far apart; the confluence of Little Bay and Oyster River spreads out blue and flat directly ahead. To retard shoreline erosion, field grass has been planted behind a fence to stabilize the tidal flat area.

Proceed to the right front corner along the shore. Here at the edge of a mature hardwood forest with shagbark hickory, maple, and oak, a sign reads Lower Walking Trail. Follow the trail, entering the woods along the salt marsh shoreline. The trail is blazed with yellow dots. Through the open patches in the woods, watch for great blue herons and yellowlegs on the hunt for mud flat creatures. The lesser and greater yellow-legs are members of the Sandpiper family, with long, stilettolike bills for digging oysters and clams—and this is Oyster River. We followed a great blue heron picking and

Wagon Hill Farm originally was an 1804 farmstead.

choosing herring and alewives in the shallows of the outgoing tide.

The trail curves right along a tidal inlet shoreline. About 0.2 mile after entering the woods, look for an impressive cluster of four large shagbark hickory trees adjacent to the trail on the left. This type of hickory can be identified by the shaggy look of its bark.

Walk up and over a slight incline and follow the trail to a Y junction 50 yards before a picnic table in the open straight ahead. Continue straight past the table onto a narrow point of land jutting into the inlet. This point provides a broad open view of Oyster River on the left and Stoney Brook Cove fed by Smith Creek on the right.

Return from the point with Stoney Brook Cove on the left and continue straight on the pathway. The trail is obvious, but look for a yellow blaze on a large red oak. Proceed down to a footbridge; in another dozen steps, turn right at a Y junction and continue onto the open grassy field path. A gravel road is straight ahead. Turn left and return to the white clapboard house, trailhead, and parking lot at the top of the hill.

Ferry Way Trail

Great Bay National Wildlife Refuge (1,054 acres)

Trip 27

Newington, New Hampshire

Distance: **2.4 miles**
Type of walk: **Loop**
Approximate time: **1 hour**
Difficulty: **Moderate**

A refuge large enough to attract bald eagles, ospreys, ravens, and herons, supporting a variety of woods and meadows.

Getting There

From the Portsmouth traffic circle where I-95 and US 1 converge, take NH 4 west and drive 1.4 miles to Exit 1 at Gosling Road. Turn left onto Gosling Road (which turns into Pease Road after the light) and drive 0.5 mile to Arboretum Drive. Turn right onto Arboretum Drive and drive 3.2 miles to the refuge parking lot on the left, across from the former Pease Air Force Base weapons storage area.

Special Features

- Observation deck on Great Bay
- Abundant seasonal wildflowers
- Nesting ospreys and bald eagles
- Close-up of a beaver pond

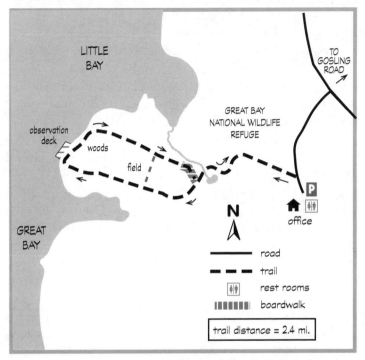

Ferry Way Trail

The sights and sounds here are plentiful and varied. The route passes through woodlands and fields, alongside a primeval-looking swamp, and overlooks a broad expanse of Great Bay. Cross Arboretum Drive to an asphalt path marked by stones that follows the chain-link fence of a former weapons compound. Friends of the Refuge is cleaning up this site, which once was a part of the Pease Air Force Base. The Great Bay National Wildlife Refuge Center was created in the late 1990s.

At 0.2 mile, cross a gravel road and follow the Ferry Way Trail sign, circling to the left on a sandy overgrown road. Black-eyed Susans, daisies, Queen Anne's lace (a member of the Parsley family), and other wildflowers grow beneath the tall sumacs with their cone-shaped berry clusters. These berry clusters often stay on the staghorn branches all winter and are a staple food for cardinals, jays, and other birds.

At 0.4 mile, shagbark hickory trees grow in the moist soil of the forest. We were surprised at the number of green-skinned hickory nuts on the trail. They are the same size and color as crab apples, which are also found on this road that once was part of a large farm.

At 0.5 mile, you approach a beaver pond that is home to a great blue heron. When we were there it flew onto a high branch of a dead tree, flapped its enormous wings, and soared away. Cattails in this pond are head-high and healthy. Older cattails turn to seed with a fluffy coating. Early colonists used to stuff mattresses with these downy seed fibers, like cotton batting.

When purple ironweed blossoms at eye level, summer is half gone; soon purple asters and tall spiked goldenrod take over. Boneset—identified by hairy opposing leaves joined at the base and small white flowers—is tall and abundant here. Penstemon, with its hairy lavender-and-yellow stamen, enjoys the moist soil here. It's nicknamed beardtongue because of its hairy stamens. Immediately after this vibrant pond, a boardwalk comes in from the right (this will be a part of the end of the loop). For now, continue on the road through the forest.

At 0.7 mile is a bench on a hill overlooking an extensive meadow. Look for the many indications that this once was a prominent farm on Great Bay. Ornamental trees—Norway spruce, silver maple, and Oriental evergreen arborvitae—often

Tiger swallowtail butterflies are abundant on Ferry Way Trail at Great Bay.

were planted near a farmhouse, along with the Japanese barberry shrub (seen along the path and identified in fall by its red-orange berries).

In another 0.2 mile, the road is bordered on each side by stone walls. Before shagbark hickory took root, open fields and pastures met the shoreline. Oddly, the land here slopes upward to Great Bay.

At 1.25 miles is an observation deck overlooking Great Bay and a trailside bench, commanding a view of the water. On the incoming tide—the most likely time to see birds on the water—gulls, ospreys, and herons wade and surf the mud flats for food.

Turn right and walk 0.1 mile until trees block the view and the trail curves away from the Great Bay basin. Far from the road, the quiet stillness of this trail is remarkable.

At 1.5 miles are some sassafras seedlings, identified by their mitten-shaped leaves. The British explorer Captain John Smith, who sailed into the harbor at Portsmouth, sent out his crew to look for sassafras, probably to be used for making a tonic or beer.

At 1.7 miles, look for the far side of the meadow you walked through earlier. One mowed path veers right through the meadow (back to the bench and ornamental trees on a hill); you walk a mowed swatch on the left edge of the meadow. To the left are swamp maples and another view of the beaver pond.

At 1.9 miles, a boardwalk crosses runoff and returns back to the road, completing the loop at the beaver pond. Turn left and backtrack the road to the sidewalk with the chain-link fence on the right.

Hours, Fees, and Facilities

An information kiosk with rest rooms is located at the entrance to the parking lot.

For More Information

Great Bay National Wildlife Refuge, 603-431-7511.

Peverly Pond Trail

Great Bay National Wildlife Refuge (1,054 acres)

Newington, New Hampshire

Distance: **0.5 mile**
Type of walk: **Loop**
Approximate time: **30 minutes**
Difficulty: **Easy**

*A graded trail through mixed forest to the open
shoreline of secluded Upper Peverly Pond.*

Getting There

From the Portsmouth traffic circle where I-95 and US 1 converge, take NH 4 west and drive 1.4 miles to Exit 1 at Gosling Road. Turn left onto Gosling Road (which turns into Pease Road after the light) and drive 0.5 mile to Arboretum Drive. Turn right onto Arboretum Drive and drive 3.2 miles to the refuge parking lot on the left, across from the former Pease Air Force Base weapons storage area.

Special Features

- Pond deck for viewing
- Boardwalks and a hard pack trail
- Universal access

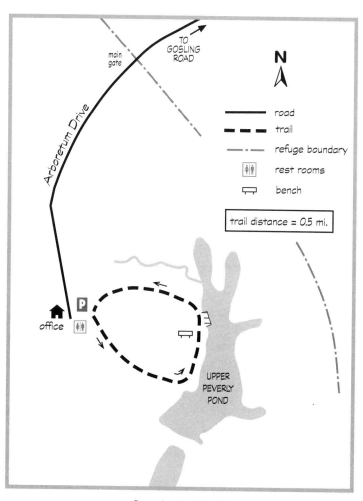

Peverly Pond Trail

At the left corner of the parking lot (facing the rest rooms and information kiosk), enter the trail through the opening in the rail fence at the Peverly Pond Trail sign. The trail combines boardwalks and hard pack dirt, making it convenient for people of all abilities. The asphalt parking lot has little to commend it, so entering the woods is a pleasant surprise. This trail attracts runners, picnickers, and office workers on coffee breaks; however, bikes, dogs, and fishing are not allowed.

The trail descends slightly at the outset and continues through an open forest of familiar New Hampshire hardwoods—maple, oak, and beech. In about 100 yards is the first of five long boardwalks situated over wet ground. On the other end of the first boardwalk over spongy earth, look to the left for club moss, a very ancient lycopsid that has lived since the first trees inhabited the earth. Club moss central spore sacs look like tiny clubs. With evergreen branchlets, club moss is sometimes called creeping cedar or ground pine. The species reproduces by spores—asexual cells that create new plants without fertilization.

In about 100 yards at the front right of the next boardwalk, we saw Indian pipes poking through the moldy leaves. Indian pipe is a pure white plant—stem, leaf, and flower are all white. The flower head hangs downward from a comparatively thick stem. This unmistakable and curious plant scarcely rises to 8 inches, living as a parasite off the decayed leaf mold and other vegetable matter in moist soil. Not surprisingly, Indian pipe is also called corpse plant or ghost flower.

The trail is easy to follow and curves left along Upper Peverly Pond at 0.2 mile. The woods are spacious here, and the pond is visible and appealing. Two benches are set in plain view. This is a "take-your-time" trail, so relax and enjoy the view.

In less than 100 yards, a small deck extends over the shore-line of this inviting, peaceful scene. To the left of the deck, where the trail curves back on the second half of its loop, beaver teeth marks are evident on two large dead tree trunks. Children can get a close-up view of the beaver's handiwork. When beavers build their dams and lodges of mud, twigs, and small branches, they fell trees near ponds and brooks with their teeth. These long teeth curve deep into their skulls to give them great chiseling power.

Near the Upper Peverly Pond shoreline where sunlight hits, we saw a black-bodied "widow skimmer" dragonfly with white-spotted wings zooming around. This pond, marshy on the far side, is home to great blue herons and belted king-fishers that hover in midflight above a fish before plunging into the pond for the capture.

A well-constructed, stone-dust trail at Peverly Pond.

At 0.3 mile, continue left at the trail sign, following a small seasonal brook. Throughout this walk, look for a variety of ferns, including the widespread bracken, stand-ing knee-high and divided into three horizontal fronds. In spring this walk provides an opportunity to see white, foamy-looking Canada mayflower and the five-petaled, fragrant pipsissewa growing from the forest floor.

At 0.51 mile on the right, the boardwalk passes by vernal pools in which tadpoles, newts, and other waterborne creatures gestate in spring.

The end point of the trail is a few yards away from the trailhead at the edge of the woods and parking lot.

Hours, Fees, and Facilities

An information kiosk with rest rooms is located at the entrance to the parking lot.

For More Information

Great Bay National Wildlife Refuge, 603-431-7511.

Cove and Border Trails

Bellamy River Audubon Wildlife Sanctuary (19 acres)

Dover, New Hampshire

Distance: **1.5 mile**
Type of walk: **Loop**
Approximate time: **45 minutes**
Difficulty: **Easy**

A bank of tidal land along the mouth of Bellamy River and a cove of Little Bay that combines intriguing examples of saltwater and freshwater ecosystems.

Getting There

At the intersection of NH 108 and US 4 in Durham, drive east on US 4 for 2.5 miles to Back River Road. Turn left onto Back River Road at the traffic light and drive 0.8 mile to Bayview Road. Turn right onto Bayview Road and drive 0.5 mile. Bear left at the Y junction onto a gravel road and drive 0.2 mile to the Audubon sign and the small parking area on the right.

Special Features

- Views of Bellamy River
- Tidal cove scenes
- River mouth at Little Bay

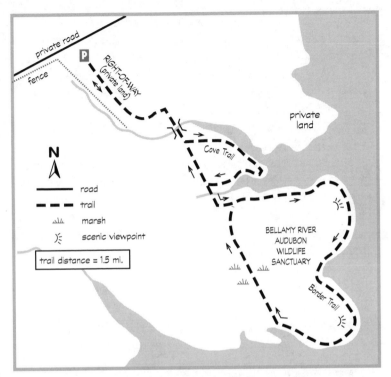

Cove and Border Trails

This wildlife sanctuary at the mouth of the Bellamy River is centrally located on the north side of Little Bay. The Piscataqua River enters from the east, and Oyster River from the west. The first facet of this walk takes you along a cove of Bellamy River, and the second offers a vantage viewing point on Little Bay.

From the parking area, walk via a right-of-way across private land, with the woods on the left and a fenced-in field on the right. In 100 yards, the Bellamy River Audubon Wildlife Sanctuary sign marks the trailhead at the end of the field boundary. Pick up a trail guide leaflet from the mailbox and enter the white pine woods. *Caution:* White pines have shallow root systems, and the roots surface in a knobby tangle on this trail, especially at the outset.

In another 100 yards, cross on the footbridge, over a rivulet. A stand of oak trees shades the area nicely. At 0.2 mile is a red-metal blaze to the left, indicating Cove Trail. Turn left onto short Cove Trail, which crosses another bridge, skirts two fingers of Bellamy River inlet, and links up with the gold-blazed Border Trail.

Here on the Cove Trail section, look for hardwoods that are not crowded by undergrowth. In spring leaf mulch under the trees provides enough moisture for a carpet of trout-lilies, with their strangely speckled leaves, as well as the drooping bell of the yellow adder's-tongue, purple and white wood violets, and the five-petaled white wood anemone. We spotted several busy bumblebees collecting nectar from these delicate early-spring bloomers.

At 0.4 mile at the junction of the Border Trail loop, bear left, keeping the river inlet to your left. The smell of the tidal flat is prominent. During summer these swampy inlets provide habitat for green and great blue herons, yellowlegs, and other waterfowl, plying the oozing mud for frogs and smaller fish.

The trail follows the border of the peninsula. This land, donated to the Audubon Society of New Hampshire by G. Allen Huggins of Dover in 1970, juts into the confluence of freshwater Bellamy River and a cove off Little Bay, which in turn flows to and from the ocean via the Piscataqua River. A daily ebb and flow of nutrients provides a rich source of food for a wide variety of coastal plants and animals, making this 10-mile-long tidal estuary a valuable environment—one of the most varied of coastal ecosystems.

Border Trail affords sparkling water views. Unfortunately, at the first outlook, the noise from Spaulding Turnpike across the inlet is inescapable. Continue skirting the shore through a stand of white birch. At 0.7 mile, the second outlook encompasses Royalls Cove to the right. At 0.8 mile, an impressively tall shagbark hickory fell recently by the trail, providing a close-up view of the peeling bark that identifies this species.

Follow the trail around the jut of land so the cove is to the left. Here in the open sweep of the tidal basin live all sorts of marine life, including flotillas of horseshoe crabs. Mature crabs

Look for bird nests in the Bellamy River Audubon Sanctuary.

shed their helmet-shaped shells. Like an invasion of amphibious tanks, horseshoe crabs drag their spiny tails across the ocean floor, while feeding from clam and oyster beds. Infuriated by these voracious armored creatures eating their steamer specials, nineteenth-century coastal farmers plowed them into their fields for fertilizer. Luckily, horseshoe crabs are as prolific as ever. In fact, their primitive but durable structure has enabled them to survive for more than 500 million years. Related to ancient sea scorpions, they are indeed living fossils.

Each spring male battalions of horseshoe crabs cling to female crabs as if they were life buoys, churning sperm over eggs as tiny and abundant as grains of sand. The infant crabs settle down to seventeen winters buried in sand and mud, waiting for another cycle to shed their shells. They feed on starfish, mussels, clams, and other tidbits unfortunate enough to be in their way.

The trail passes through a beech grove. The Border Trail loop ends at 1.2 miles. Turn left and follow the gold blazes for the return trip. After crossing the two footbridges, exit the wood with the fenced-in field now on the left and walk to the parking area.

A word of comfort: Sea breezes and salt air seem to discourage New Hampshire blackflies in spring (between early May and mid-June), although water birds are easier to spot between July and September.

Fort Trail

Fort McClary State Park

Kittery, Maine

Distance: **0.3 mile**
Type of walk: **Loop**
Approximate time: **30 minutes**
Difficulty: **Easy**

*Unique views of the mouth of the Piscataqua River, Whaleback
Light, the U.S. Coast Guard Lighthouse, and the Isles of Shoals.*

Getting There

From I-95, take ME 103 east to Kittery center. From the Kittery
Public Library, drive east past Portsmouth Naval Shipyard at
0.4 mile and Lady Pepperrell Home at 1.7 miles. At 2.0 miles,
you come to the Fort McClary sign on the right with a large
parking lot near the site. The site is open from June through
August for car parking, but walkers can enter in the off-season.

Special Features

- Former military blockhouse
- Strategic views of Piscataqua River
- Civil War–era underground "caponier" shooting tunnel

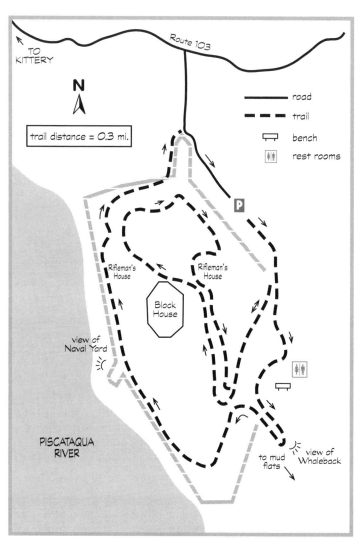

TO
KITTERY

Route 103

N

trail distance = 0.3 mi.

—————— road

– – – – trail

bench

rest rooms

P

Rifleman's
House

Rifleman's
House

Block
House

view of
Naval Yard

PISCATAQUA
RIVER

view of
Whaleback

to mud
flats

Fort Trail

This small, important historical site provided coastal defense during the Revolutionary War, the War of 1812, the Civil War, the Spanish-American War, and World War I. Situated at the mouth of the Piscataqua River, the fort offers walkers an ideal view of the lay of the land and water at this gateway between Maine and New Hampshire.

The first fort on this site was built by William Pepperrell, an early resident, during the Indian skirmishes in 1690. The Pepperrell fort was more of a garrison—a strategically positioned house surrounded by a stockade behind which colonists could take refuge during a siege. The only time Fort McClary was really pressed into service was during the Spanish-American War in 1898, during which three large cannons were trained on the river.

For a 0.3-mile loop of the site, begin at the parking lot inside the grounds. Walk straight past the rest rooms on the left beneath a group of white pines and down the incline past some of the granite blocks measuring 9 feet by 3 feet. Fort McClary's granite walls, or "flanks," were added to the original Block House, built in 1844, about twenty years later, but this flank next to the parking lot was never completed. Possibly these granite blocks were off-loaded from a gundalow—a river barge that originated in Portsmouth.

If the tide is out, you will see more chunks of granite, feldspar, quartz, and other geological remains deposited by a glacier that moved across the sand and clay beds during the last ice age. Anchored to them is the ubiquitous bladder wrack; buoyant, fingertip-size air sacs allow this seaweed to float to the surface on the incoming tide.

The shore is precipitous, and if you have younger children along, take them up to the fenced-in parapet. In military terms, this was the earthwork and cannon battery. Directly across the river is the U.S. Coast Guard Lighthouse in Newcastle on Great Island (the site of Portsmouth's first fort), and directly in front of you, in midriver, is Whaleback Light. Both the Coast Guard station and lighthouse are still in operation. About 9 miles east in the distance, visible on a clear day, are many of the nine Isles of Shoals (see walk 16). If you'd like to view these features in more detail, look through a mounted pair of binoculars on the parapet.

To the west of Fort McClary is Portsmouth Naval Shipyard. On this same site American ships of mast pine (like the tall white pines you see at the gate to the site) were built for the British Navy in the early 1700s. Today, the shipyard is a world-

Directly across the Piscataqua River from Kittery, Maine, stands the U.S. Coast Guard Lighthouse at Newcastle, New Hampshire.

class producer of nuclear submarines. Within the protection of the massive wall, a jungle of sumac and other marginal plants have taken root.

Walking along the periphery with the river on your left, you come to a jutting tunnel-like structure called a caponier. Built originally of brick during the Civil War, it permitted soldiers to place and sight their guns in all directions along the wall.

Continue upriver on the granite walk until you reach the granite wall flanking the western side of the fort. At a low-slung clump of juniper bushes, veer to your right onto the grass sward. Lowbush juniper thrives in harsh weather. It's prickly with tenacious roots that make this hardy evergreen a useful landscaping plant to check soil erosion. Its bluish green cones take three seasons to mature. Skirt the periphery of the fort, climbing the grassy incline between the western wall and natural slate-clay rock embankment.

At 0.2 mile, notice an old apple tree rooted in the jagged stone bank. Nestled in the chiseled nooks and crannies are stonecrop plants, which produce clusters of minute white flowers in spring; they can be identified by their oval toothed leaves.

A second caponier tunnel front may be entered by steps inside the fort wall.

Having walked the periphery, head east, back through the parking lot, and this time ascend the steep asphalt path to the Block House, perched atop another granite-walled earthwork. The roofless building on the right had a twin on the opposite side (now a barely visible foundation) and was used by riflemen defending the flank.

Circle around the back of the Block House past the Magazine, where gunpowder was kept dry. Built in 1808, this brick building predates all others currently on this site.

Three flights of steps located directly behind the Block House (closed to public) lead to the pentagonal-shaped granite caponier. Descend the fort hill and return to the parking lot. A park with picnic tables is located across the road on Spruce Creek.

For More Information

Fort McClary State Historic Site, 28 Oldfields Road, South Berwick, ME 03908; 207-384-5160.

Shoreline Trail

Fort Foster
(89 acres)
Kittery Point, Maine

Distance: **0.75 mile**
Type of walk: **Loop**
Approximate time: **45 minutes**
Difficulty: **Easy**

*A wonderful walk along a rocky shoreline past a
cattail marsh, black sand beaches, and a view
of the Isles of Shoals 9 miles away on the horizon.*

Getting There

From the Kittery Public Library, drive 3 miles east on ME 103 to
the Y junction of Chauncey Creek Road. Following signs to Fort
Foster, turn right onto Chauncey Creek Road, cross the bridge
over Chauncey Creek, and at 3.5 miles turn right onto Pocahontas Road. Follow Pocahontas Road for 1.2 miles to the park
gatehouse at 4.7 miles. If the gate is closed, use a pass-through
gate open for walkers in the off-season. Park at the Pier Parking
Lot to the left of the beach area on the Piscataqua River.

Special Features

• Spectacular river and ocean views
• Multiple swamp, woodland, and shore habitats
• Tidal pools

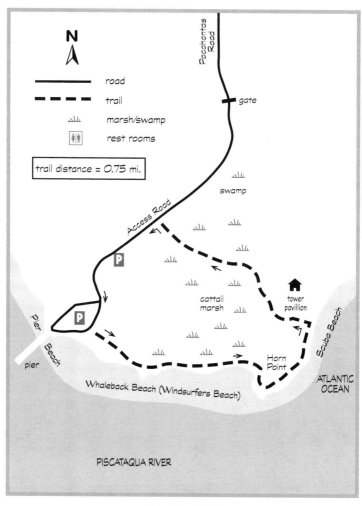

N

——————	road
- - - - -	trail
⟋⟍⟋	marsh/swamp
🚻	rest rooms

trail distance = 0.75 mi.

Pocohontas Road

gate

swamp

Access Road

P

cattail marsh

tower pavillion

P

Pier Beach

pier

Horn Point

Scuba Beach

ATLANTIC OCEAN

Whaleback Beach (Windsurfers Beach)

PISCATAQUA RIVER

Shoreline Trail

A view of Whaleback Lighthouse from the Shoreline Trail.

Situated at Kittery Point at the entrance to Portsmouth Harbor, Fort Foster on Gerrish Island was built in 1872 to protect Portsmouth and its strategic location at the mouth of the Piscataqua River between New Hampshire and Maine. When World War II began, Fort Foster was expanded to guard the harbor where the Portsmouth Naval Shipyard built warships and submarines. The town of Kittery now owns the fort; its grounds are a public recreational park.

The trailhead is located to the left (east) of the Pier Parking Lot as you face the Piscataqua River. Enter the wide, dirt trail, marked at the start by two small boulders with saplings and staghorn sumac on both sides.

Walk a few yards over a slight incline, and suddenly an open ledge comes into view, with the Isles of Shoals (see walk

16) visible in the distance. On a clear day at high tide, you might enjoy trying to identify some of the nine Isles of Shoals —Appledore, Star (the largest), Smuttynose, White Island (with the lighthouse), and the smaller islands, Lunging, Cedar, Duck, Malaga, and Seavey.

Along this pathway are classic Maine sights and smells—a rough, rocky shoreline, saltwater spray, lighthouses, abandoned wharf pilings, pungent sea wrack, and fragrant beach roses. Many benches are placed in key spots along the trail. The pebble beach with steel-gray granite sand—so-called black sand— is thick with oval stones worn smooth by relentless wave action. On the right between the shore and the trail grows golden tansy, a member of the Aster family. Blooming in early fall, tansy has small yellow flowers in flat, round clusters that in early American farmhouse kitchens were used in tansy cakes. Chopped tansy leaves also were used in tea, to spark up puddings, flavor omelets, and enhance stews and salads.

A short distance ahead, at 150 yards into the walk, Kittery Point offers a good look at Whaleback Lighthouse on an island, guarding the entrance to Portsmouth Harbor.

On the left behind the beach is a cattail marsh extending all the way to the access road. If you take a very short side trail, you can view this extensive marsh of several acres. Most likely, you will encounter red-winged blackbirds and catbirds calling and flitting about. Catbirds make a trademark soft *mewing* sound that gives this Thrush family member its name. These long-tailed, gray birds with black caps mimic other birds in a rambling bird bedlam.

At 0.2 mile, the marsh ends where a sign is posted that reads Shoreline Walk. Walk up the steps to a secluded overlook from Horn Point of the mouth of the Piscataqua River flowing out past Portsmouth to the west and of Kittery Point due east. The Shoreline Trail then turns northward and leads you along a stretch with dramatic views of shoreline ledges. At 0.3 mile, you'll reach a bench backed by thickets and facing the Isles of Shoals.

This section of beach and rock outcroppings traps salt water at the intertidal zone. Exploring tide pools can turn up any number of fascinating marine flora and fauna, including blue mussels, which attach in clumps by threads among seaweed on rocks and pilings. Children might also discover the hermit crab, which lives only in empty shells; the shell-less crabs move into new housing units as they grow larger.

At 0.4 mile, with a handsome cluster of golden birch trees ahead, you can either return on the same trail along the shore or walk toward the open-air Tower Pavilion, visible on the left, which avoids the vast cattail marsh stretching nearly to the parking area. The Tower Pavilion, which you pass on your right, was used during World War II for bunkers. It has since been transformed into a public shelter for large picnics, with tables beneath the roof and on the lawn.

At the top of the rise, descend on the paved road and pass the cattail marsh on your left. Turn left on the park access road and walk 0.25 mile back to the parking area beside small birches, hemlocks, pussywillows, and sandbar willows.

Wiggly Bridge Trail
Steedman Woods (16 acres)

York, Maine

Distance: **0.75 mile**
Type of walk: **Loop**
Approximate time: **30–45 minutes**
Difficulty: **Easy**

A short urban trail on a peninsula between York Harbor and a tide pond accessed by "the world's smallest suspension bridge."

Getting There

From the visitor center on US 1 in York, turn left onto York Street and drive 0.2 mile. Turn right onto Organug Road and drive 0.9 mile. Take Seabury Road across the bridge and drive 1.0 mile. Turn left (east) onto ME 103, drive 0.8 mile, and cross a bridge back over the York River. You'll see Wiggly Bridge on your left in the distance. Parking spaces on the right give access to the historical Sayward-Wheeler House and Fisherman's Walk (see walk 33). Built in 1718 by Jonathan Sayward, this prominent riverview house is open for tours from June through October.

Special Features

- World's smallest pedestrian suspension bridge
- Views of Barrells Mill Pond and York Harbor
- Rhododendron grove

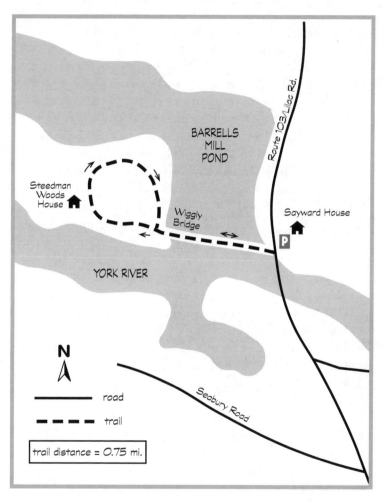

Wiggly Bridge Trail

This historical bridge, built in 1936, crosses a dammed outlet of Barrells Mill Pond, formed by a crescent-shaped earthen levee topped with gravel. Cross ME 103 (Lilac Road). The walk starts at a 200-yard levee, which leads to Wiggly Bridge and a small wooded preserve. The nature preserve was given to The Old York Historical Society by Charles Richard Steedman "to be kept forever wild for the enjoyment of the residents of York."

This tidal millpond was created by a dam in 1726. Nineteen citizens of York organized and built the dam to run lumber and gristmills by an ingenious underwater waterwheel system.

As you walk the 200 yards toward the bridge, the working harbor on your left and the millpond on your right demonstrate that tidal power was free and effective for merchants and farmers. Today, you can see the great power of the tide surging beneath the bridge through the narrow opening in the dam, and imagine this waterpower turning millstones.

The mill wasn't the only enterprise at this site. In the 1880s, ice blocks were cut from the millpond with long saws, loaded onto gundalow barges, and shipped by sea to Boston and other destinations. The ice blocks also were hauled by horses and oxen and stored in barns and sheds. Ice covered with sawdust for insulation was stored throughout the summer, keeping perishables cool.

Once across the bridge, you can walk down a few stone steps to cleared beach areas on either side along the York River. Or continue along the trail, soon reaching a Y junction with the loop around Steedman Woods. Go straight on the wider trail, taking your time as you enter the woods with the York River and the harbor on your left. A slower pace is not only more relaxing but also puts you more in touch with the casual

The world's smallest suspension bridge, "Wiggly" stretches over the outlet of a 1726 millpond to a bird sanctuary.

rhythms here. You'll end up seeing more details of both the natural and human-made landscape.

On your left, just after a prickly barberry bush, are long-stemmed buttercups; these bloom in early summer with shiny, inch-wide, deep yellow flowers. Small sections of thin woods and brush open onto the harbor as you stroll on this earthen trail. Notice how waterlines on the shore marking spring tides (flood tides at full moon) are visible high on the banks.

For a preserve known as a bird sanctuary, we didn't notice that many birds when we walked here. A York historian and birder we spoke with has seen a worrisome reduction in birds around York in recent decades. In part, she attributes the decrease to developmental sprawl on the coastal flyway—reducing feeding and nesting areas for birds and insects. Bear right at the private residence. The trail runs parallel to a row of rhododendron bushes, with scarlet and magenta blooms from late May to early June.

At 0.3 mile is a Y junction. Turn right and the tide pond will be on your left.

The heavily used trail splits again, this time into several branches all heading back to the bridge. Make your way on the lower shore path where bluets and lilies carpet a grove of birches. At 0.5 mile, the trail narrows and Wiggly Bridge reappears. Return to the parking area by crossing the bridge and earthen levee.

Fisherman's Walk

York Harbor

York, Maine

Distance: **1.6 miles**
Type of walk: **Out-and-back**
Approximate time: **1 hour**
Difficulty: **Easy**

An in-town walk along a busy working harbor with fishing boats, piers, and delightfully landscaped residential gardens.

Getting There

From the visitor center in York (on US 1 off I-95), turn left onto York Street and drive 0.2 mile. Turn right onto Organug Street and drive 0.9 mile, crossing the bridge over the York River. Just over the bridge, turn left onto Seabury Road and drive 1.0 mile. Turn left onto ME 103 and drive 0.8 mile back toward York and back across the York River. On the other side of the bridge on the right is a parking area for the Wiggly Bridge (see walk 32) and Fisherman's Walk.

Special Features

- Harborside walkway
- Landscaped residences overlooking the harbor
- Lively private and commercial harbor
- Historic Sayward-Wheeler estate

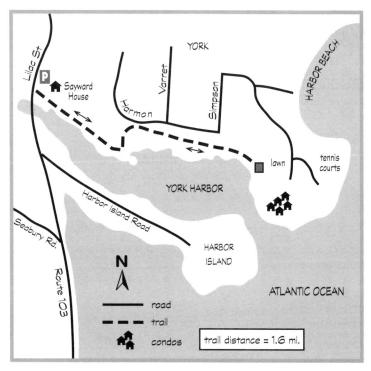

Fisherman's Walk

The land for Fisherman's Walk was donated by private citizens, and indeed it is a wondrous gift to stroll this path beside the tidal York River. When the tide is out, gulls, yellowlegs, and other "waders" forage the mud flats for clams and mussels. At high tide, the water lilts against the docks and wharves.

    The town walk is on a sidewalk and a dirt path. It begins to the right of the parking area just behind a high hedge on the historic Sayward-Wheeler estate. Jonathan Sayward (1713–97), a prominent York probate judge, also owned a fleet of six commercial sloops that sailed in and out of York Harbor, exporting ship masts of tall white pine to England and importing goods from the West Indies.

A stone seawall fronts York River and York Harbor, which continues as a busy fishing and lobstering port. You'll be passing several commercial piers on the walk.

Steps along the river lead to a narrow asphalt alley. Follow this alley and, at 0.2 mile on the left, you can't miss the huge trunk of a silver maple big enough for half a dozen children with arms stretched wide to form a ring around the trunk. This

Fisherman's Walk passes a marina, commercial docks, fishing boats, and historic houses at York Harbor.

magnificent tree grows leaves—silvery underneath—that are much more deeply lobed than the familiar sugar maple. Pass through a gate at the end of the alley; a sign indicating that the land for Fisherman's Walk was "given by the generosity of private citizens" marks the beginning of Fisherman's Walk.

In the harbor and river lobster boats, kayaks, and sailing yachts glide by as you walk in the shade of grandfather trees. A hedge of spring lilacs wafts its fragrance in the sea breeze, and song sparrows serenade in the tangled (and tenacious) cover of barberry, Japanese honeysuckle, and beach roses. At 0.4 mile, we were glad to see a fine, elderly elm that had escaped the devastating plague of Dutch elm disease, which since the 1920s has killed many of these magnificent fountain-branched trees across America. The gray bark of American elm has narrow, vertical ridges; the narrow heart-shaped leaves grow from fountainlike sprays of branches. Fortunately, disease-resistant strains of elms are available. We saw some these saplings growing in a park farther up the coast.

Beyond the pier and to the left, high on an embankment of daisies and phlox, is a stand of black locust. Black locust trees crown high and have deep-ridged, often curvy black trunks; their frondlike leaves provide a light, airy canopy.

At 0.5 mile, a tall, bushy ornamental spruce towers near the river path just beyond a second private pier. At 0.6 mile, a building on a pier interrupts Fisherman's Walk. Veer left and cross the fisherman's alley back onto a sidewalk. Continue the walk along a beautifully landscaped walled garden with a railing on your right. In season, the peonies, irises, and ornamental flowers are an exquisite feast for eyes and nose.

Follow the river road alongside another stone wall with the river on the right until you come to a wide lawn marked with another Fisherman's Walk sign at 0.8 mile. Officially, this is where the walk terminates. Retracing your steps will bring you back to the beginning of the walk. Before you return you can cross the lawn to the left (the path to the right is private), where there is a town park and the pebble cove of York Harbor Beach.

Nubble Trail
and Nubble Light

Sohier Park, Cape Neddick (3 acres)

York, Maine

Distance: **0.5 mile**
Type of walk: **Loop**
Approximate time: **30 minutes**
Difficulty: **Easy**

*A historical, picturesque lighthouse on an island close
to a rocky shoreline park and viewpoint.*

Getting There

From the visitor center at the junction of US 1 and I-95 in York,
drive south one block and turn east onto ME 1A. Drive 5.0
miles on ME 1A through York Village. Just past Long Sands
Beach (before York Beach), turn right onto Nubble Road.
Drive 1.0 mile to Sohier Park on the point of Cape Neddick
and park on the right near the welcome center.

Special Features

- Classic old lighthouse complex
- Extensive rock ledges
- Long north and south coastline views

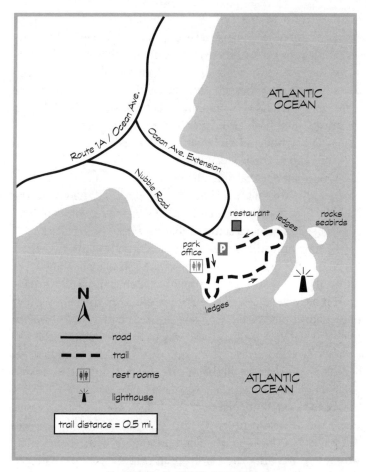

Nubble Trail and Nubble Light

At Cape Neddrick, red-and-white Nubble Lighthouse was built in 1879 on tiny Nubble Island, a very short distance from the mainland. "Nubble Light" is one of the most photographed lighthouses in Maine. Visitors can park and walk the rugged shoreline at Sohier Park directly opposite the famed lighthouse.

With your back to the welcome center, turn right and walk down the lawn to a small enclave of memorial rocks. Between them, a path cuts through wildflowers to sun-bleached granite ledges and splendid views looking south onto the open Atlantic. In spring, blue flags (wild irises) grow among the tall grasses, along with cinquefoil (five-petaled flowers) and some poison ivy—so keep to the trodden path.

One staffer at the welcome center told us that she and her brother used to walk from Long Sands Beach all the way to the Nubble. Now much of the land is private, and recently an over-size house has blocked some of the view from Sohier Park.

Return from the ledges to the main path along the shore, keeping to the right of the parking area. Coin-operated binoculars are available if you forgot to bring yours. Behemoth boulders have broken off, and geysers of ocean spray spill over the ledges sailors once named Savage Rocks. Here on the point you do have an unobstructed view south, all the way to Kittery Point on the Pis-cataqua River bordering New Hampshire. Looking northeast, on a clear day you can see all the way to Moody Point and beyond to Kennebunkport.

Focus your binoculars on the ledges north of the pictur-esque nineteenth-century lighthouse, and most likely you will see black sea ducks and a few cormorants with spread-eagle wings. Cormorants are spectacular black seabirds with S-shaped necks and wings that measure nearly a yard tip to tip. Adult cormorants often have colorful faces with orange beaks, green eyes, a double crest, and a gular (throat) pouch where fish are stored before being swallowed.

Between the Nubble and the mainland at Sohier Park

you'll notice a cable strung across the boat channel from a high, steel structure on the island to a similar structure on the mainland point. Although most of the bluff is part of Sohier Park, this contraption and the Nubble Light (automated in 1987) are under the purview of the U.S. Coast Guard. A dinghylike car swings from the cable and provides electrically powered transportation across the channel and through the air for lighthouse maintenance.

Continue circling the point to three granite benches and another pair of coin-operated binoculars on the northwest side of the Neddick peninsula. Walk the road 0.1 mile and then descend a gradual incline onto pink granite ledges. High surf leaves tide pools that grow brackish under the summer sun. But children find them fascinating, and you may find strands of seaweed and brine shrimp.

Although invisible, up to 50,000 krill may inhabit a cubic meter of water. These shrimplike crustaceans are what blue, humpback, finback, and minke whales siphon through their baleen—fringed bones that sieve food from the ocean. More than likely, you'll see the common amphipods called sideswimmers and scuds—both related to those annoying sand-hopping fleas.

This rock platform is geologically interesting. Walk down to a ridge of tumbled sea boulders, and on closer examination you'll see that they're riddled with pockmarks. During volcanic activity molten lava flowed around smaller pebbles, causing the pitting, as with a mold. Return to the road and a fifth granite bench overlooking more ledges. From here you can see two veins of white quartzite running through these compressed granite ledges, another example of volcanic layering.

At 0.4 mile, continue past the Sohier Park Ordinance sign to an untouched, fenced-in natural grassland of cattails and

"The Savage Rocks" and popular Nubble Light at Cape Neddick.

beach roses. Although small, the patch of growth provides cover for songbirds.

If children are on the walk, hold their hands while crossing the road back to the welcome center and a bell cast in 1926. The booming bell warned mariners of the "Savage Rocks" surrounding this point of Cape Neddick. The bell hung from a pyramidal structure attached to the tower and was operated by a clocklike mechanism during low visibility but has been replaced by a power-operated foghorn.

Ring and Blueberry Bluff Trails

Mount Agamenticus (7,000 acres)

York, Maine

Trip 35

Distance: **1.8 miles**
Type of walk: **Out-and-back**
Approximate time: **1 hour**
Difficulty: **Moderate**

A climb through mixed woods past ledge outlooks to the 691-foot summit for distant views of the Atlantic coast.

Getting There

From the Greater York Region Chamber of Commerce Visitor Center at US 1 and I-95, drive north on US 1 for 4 miles. Turn left (at Flo's Hot Dog stand, on the right) onto Mountain Road, and drive 1.5 miles to a stop sign. Turn right onto Mountain Road and drive 2.7 miles to the Mount Agamenticus access road on the right. Turn onto this road and drive 0.2 mile to the first small parking lot on the left, at the sign for the Ring Trail.

Special Features

- Views from ledges halfway up trail
- Summit plaque honoring the Abenaki saint Aspinquid
- Mountaintop lodge

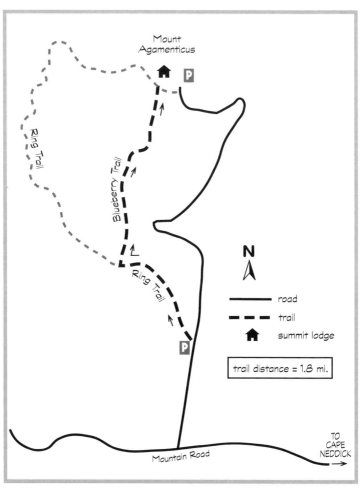

Mount
Agamenticus

Ring Trail

Blueberry Trail

Ring Trail

N

road
trail
summit lodge

trail distance = 1.8 mi.

TO
CAPE
NEDDICK

Mountain Road

Ring and Blueberry Bluff Trails

Mount Agamenticus is a monadnock, the highest point in York County and a salient landmark. This multiuse, large mountain park is owned by nine public and private organizations for hiking, mountain biking, horseback riding, and all-terrain vehicles (ATVs). The town of York owns the crown of 180 acres. Trails are designated for various recreational activities; a few are designated for hiking only. A lodge at the summit may be rented for family picnics, gatherings, and group programs.

Two boulders mark the Ring trailhead directly in front of the parking area. (You can pick up a map in the map box made by Boy Scout Troop 301.) Enter a hemlock forest. The first 100 yards or so are flat and marked with white blazes. In spring, runoff water crosses the trail in spots, and in 300 yards a brook may seep onto the trail. At this time of year the hemlocks have a chartreuse growth on the branch tips.

At a Y junction, veer right and start climbing the slope. As always on mountain trails, be aware of rocks and roots underfoot, although the overlooks and wildflowers may hold your attention.

Soon you'll come to signs for Ring Trail and Blueberry Bluff Trail. Take the red-blazed Blueberry Bluff Trail to the right and ascend. Now you're on the mountainside.

Several multiuse trails lead to the summit of Mt. Agamenticus.

It's not strenuous, however, and given the elevation of Mount A (as it's sometimes called), the exertion is not prolonged.

You soon arrive at ledges covered with lowbush blueberries. After an open rocky stretch is a steep, short incline and a second series of open ledges at 0.4 mile. Lowbush and highbush blueberries are shrubs related to huckleberries and cranberries, all members of the Heath family (Ericaceae).

At the second set of ledges is an unlimited view of the forested southern Maine countryside. Sometimes walkers miss these wide-open views because of an iron resolve to reach the summit, but during summer this view is better than the view from the top (which is blocked by foliage until late fall).

In spring you'll see bridal wreath and lady's slippers (a showy member of the Orchid family) at 0.4 mile alongside the trail. Blueberry Bluff—about halfway up the mountain at 0.5 mile—offers another long view, which includes the White Mountains of New Hampshire.

The trail curves back into a grove of white pines and oaks. Whalebacks of granite surface here as you continue upward. In spring we spotted a mourning cloak butterfly with dark brown wings outlined in gold fluttering through the open section.

At 0.7 mile, you'll reach a Y junction. Blueberry Bluff Trail continues right, but this short leg of the trail may be closed; if so, take the left fork. Either trail soon deposits you at a T junction with Horse Trail (marked by a trail post).

Fifty yards more and you can see the "aerial tower" on Mount Agamenticus. Straight ahead is the summit lodge to the far side of the access road and gravel parking area. A large plaque near the summit parking lot honors Saint Aspinquid, an Abenaki Indian medicine man who converted to Christianity.

When he died in 1682 at age ninety-four, Native Americans from a radius of 100 miles arrived to pay homage. It was said that 6,723 wild animals were sacrificed at this spot to honor him. His grave was covered with stones so wolves wouldn't dig up the remains. A custom continues to this day for each visitor to add a stone to the pile.

Return by the same route.

River Run Trail
and Bridle Path

Vaughan Woods State Park (250 acres)

South Berwick, Maine

Distance: **2.0 miles**
Type of walk: **Loop**
Approximate time: **2 hours**
Difficulty: **Moderate**

A forest of venerable white pines and hemlocks in
an inland preserve on Salmon Falls River.

Getting There

From the junction of ME 91 and ME 236 in South Berwick, drive north on ME 236 for 0.7 mile. At the Vaughan Woods State Park sign, turn left onto Old Fields Road. Travel for 1.0 mile to the state park entrance on the right and continue to a picnic area parking lot with rest rooms.

Special Features

- Majestic 90- to 100-foot Eastern white pines and old hemlocks
- Historical Hamilton House
- Benches overlooking Salmon Falls River

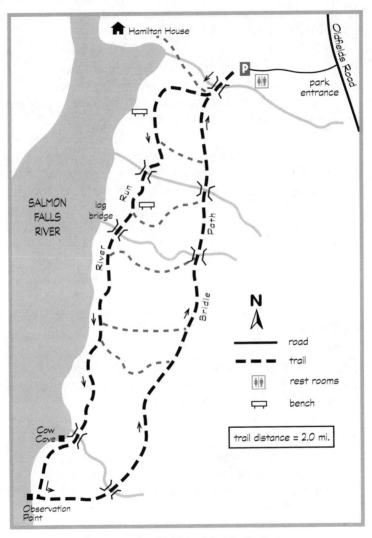

River Run Trail and Bridle Path

If you've had enough of vacation beach sitting, this walk is shaded and cool—a good outing on hot, summery days. You'll be walking along a wide pathway through a mature forest stand of Eastern white pine and hemlock. The magnificent Eastern white pines are the largest conifers (cone-bearing trees) in the Northeast and favor moist, porous soil. Virgin stands like this provided the British with 100-foot masts for their sailing fleets.

The trail begins behind the information kiosk at an opening in the woods at the far end of the parking area near the picnic area. After descending a short distance, cross over a brook using the footbridge. In about 80 yards, the trail veers to the right.

At a three-trail junction, take the middle trail—River Run Trail (the Bridle Path Trail is on the left, and the Hamilton House trail leading through two granite fence posts is on the right). In about 200 yards on the right, Salmon Falls River flows south on its way to the Piscataqua River.

In another 50 yards, a Shady Stroll trail sign appears near a platform and bench overlooking Salmon Falls River with a view of Hamilton House to the north. The hip-roofed Federal-style house, built in 1785 by the shipbuilding Hamilton family, was restored in 1898 by Emily Tyson. Today the public may tour the historical house and grounds overlooking the river.

Return to River Run Trail and continue south through woods that evoke the quiet grandeur of early America, with giant white pines reaching skyward like cathedral spires.

The trail is generally well maintained, although tree roots occasionally protrude into the path. The roots are dabbed with neon-colored paint, alerting people to use caution.

Walk over a series of small footbridges. The sloping terrain on the left undulates and descends into gullies and sometimes-muddy ground at shoreline. (If time is limited, you can take Windy Walk/Old Gate Trail and loop back to the trailhead.)

At about 0.5 mile, descend to a high footbridge with railings. Do not climb the knoll to the left after the bridge; instead, continue along the river. The trail will become more obvious as you follow the shore. (If you get to a junction at the top to find you've taken Nubble Knoll Trail, turn right and descend this connector trail back to the river.)

At 0.75 mile, another series of wood and stone footbridges have been built over an intriguing tangle of tree roots. The trail comes out of a short bend in the trail onto Cow Cove. In 1634 the first cows in this region were carried and off-loaded here by a ship appropriately named the *Pied Cow*.

The historic 1785 Hamilton House on the tidal Salmon River in Vaughan Woods.

In another 0.1 mile is the Trails End sign. Here, a bench allows you to rest and contemplate the river before looping back.

The second part of the walk is on the wide Bridle Path, leading east away from the river. From the junction (clearly marked with a sign), ascend through a mixed deciduous forest of maple and birch. In this upland section, there are numerous birds, wood ferns, wildflowers, and intermittent sunny clearings. Towhees, blue jays, hermit thrushes, orioles, and many other northern birds flit through the foliage of tall American white ash.

At 1.4 miles, a sign on the left identifies the Warren Homesite. James Warren, a Scot born in 1620, arrived in the New World in 1650 as a prisoner from the Battle of Dunbar. He settled here with his wife in 1656. Several trails join the Bridle Path. At 1.5 miles, Nubble Knoll Trail enters from the left. Then at 1.7 miles, Windy Walk cross trail joins on the left, followed by Porcupine Path a short distance beyond.

Continue on the Bridle Path. At 1.9 miles is the junction with River Run Trail where you began your loop walk. Continue right to cross the footbridge, and ascend the slope to the parking lot and picnic area.

For More Information

Vaughan Woods State Park, 28 Oldfields Road, South Berwick, ME 03908; park season: 207-384-5160; off-season: 207-624-6080.

Marginal Way Foot Path
Ogunquit Marina

Ogunquit, Maine

Distance: **1.5 miles**
Type of walk: **Out-and-back**
Approximate time: **1 hour**
Difficulty: **Easy**

This cliffside footpath along a craggy shoreline is one of the most popular walkways on the north Atlantic coast.

Getting There

From US 1 at the three-way junction with Beach Road in downtown Ogunquit, drive 1.2 miles on Shore Road to the marina inlet and parking lot. The Marginal Way trailhead is to the left of the parking entrance. The access road leads to more metered parking spaces and public rest rooms along Perkins Cove, a picturesque working harbor with shops and galleries.

Special Features

- Easy all the way for all ages
- Paved trail, benches, lookouts
- Wonderful 180-degree ocean views
- Interesting geological features, including a boar's head and trap dikes
- Universally accessible

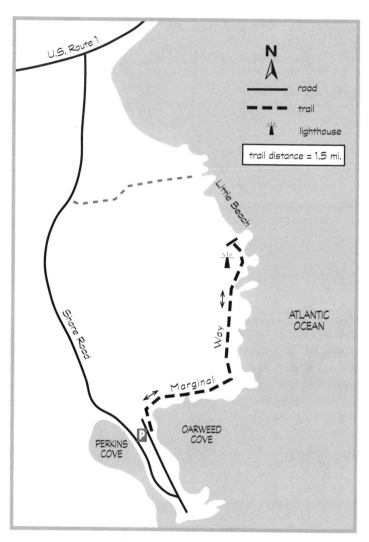

Marginal Way Foot Path

Marginal Way offers spectacular shoreline vistas from a rounded promontory extending north to the Ogunquit River.

At the entrance to the main parking lot, look for the Marginal Way Foot Path sign to the left in front on the ocean side of the restaurant entrance. A colorful combination of roses and pink granite boulders marks the trailhead. The footpath makes a gradual incline up to a dramatic perch above the crashing surf.

Grasses, flowers, shrubs, and trees grow profusely on both sides of the trail. The fast-growing, non-native Japanese honeysuckle vine (which can grow 30 feet in a year and doesn't yield much of a scent) has taken over in some spots. Hobblebush (also in the Honeysuckle family) produces a "bridal wreath" circlet of flowers, which turn into red berries. The berries turn blue-black in the fall. Be aware that poison ivy flourishes on the sunlit borders of the trail.

Walk uphill through Atlantic white cedar and brush before the trail levels off.

At 0.2 mile, cross a wooden footbridge, where you can see a good example of a trap dike—a chutelike break in the rocky earth. The waves crash between the dark, rugged, granite walls. Wave action and spray are especially exciting as the tide comes in.

Trap dikes along Marginal Way are chutelike breaks in the geological formation that create dramatic upsurges of shore waves.

Marginal Way follows the edge of a residential section, but you won't see any houses on the left until about 0.25 mile. For the most part, houses and walkers are hidden by trees and shrubbery.

At 0.3 mile, you can see a "boar's head"—a name coined by early settlers for this type of rocky jut of land on the coast. This boar's head is fairly open, with a stunted grove of low sumac.

Curve around this thrusting cliff topped with low juniper shrubs. Quarter-inch juniper cones are often called "berries" when sold as condiments for stews—and gin.

Marginal Way makes a tight turn, and at nearly 0.5 mile on the right is another trap dike (a green chain-link fence shields walkers from a precipitous cliffside). This last part of the trail provides panoramic views of new building developments in Ogunquit. A short distance ahead on your left a bronze plaque reads: "Recent studies by the Maine State Planning Office project the entire Maine coast will be developed to the Canadian border by 2050 unless urban sprawl is held in check."

The trail curves around another wide trap dike (with houses now on your left), and you come to a large bronze memorial dedicated to the hundred volunteers who helped restore Marginal Way after the storm of October 31, 1991. Continue along the footpath, which gradually descends to water level. Residences now are clearly visible to the left.

A large replica of a lighthouse indicates the end of this walk. A sign on the lighthouse by the Marginal Way Restoration Committee reads: "Marginal Way presented to Ogunquit Village Corporation by the Hon. Josiah Chase of York, Maine 1925. Enjoy our inspiring Marginal Way. Your generous donations help us maintain and improve it. We are most grateful." Return by the same route.

Footbridge Beach Trail

Ogunquit River and Beach

Ogunquit, Maine

Trip 38

Distance: **1 mile**
Type of walk: **Loop**
Approximate time: **1 hour**
Difficulty: **Easy**

A walkers' wooden bridge across sand dunes to the ocean beach and back along the Ogunquit River tidal flats.

Getting There

From Ogunquit Center (junction of Beach Road and US 1), drive north on US 1 for 1.1 miles. Turn right onto Ocean Street and drive east 0.4 mile to the Footbridge Beach parking lot.

Special Features

- Dunes with American beach grass
- Broad Atlantic shore views
- Sandpipers, egrets, and other shorebirds

Walking Ogunquit Beach is like walking into an abstract painting with long horizon lines. Many painters, in fact, live here. Behind you, to the east, is Moody Point in Wells, and before you is a "boar's head," a term early settlers gave to cliff outcrops.

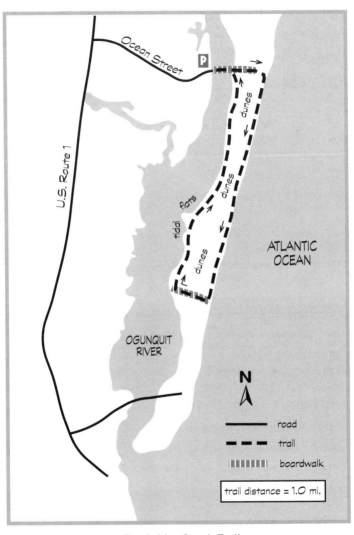

Footbridge Beach Trail

This boar's head is completely covered now with new development. But down on the beach, only the sound of surf greets you, and beachgoers' colorful kites sail the currents with the seagulls.

The tidal Ogunquit River makes a U-turn at the mouth and runs parallel to the fine, light sand of Ogunquit Beach. Maps of this popular walk show the footbridge over the river to the beach. But because maps aren't geological, a major feature has been left out—the sand dunes between the river and beach. This is a fine example of a barrier beach.

Be sure to check the tidal chart for Ogunquit and arrive within an hour before or after low tide. If the tide is high, you won't be able to walk along the river. We recommend light rubber-soled beach shoes that can be removed for the beach part of the loop but will come in handy on the shell-littered mud flats of the river.

The trail begins at the pedestrian bridge, which arcs over the wide river and provides a broad view upstream and down. Swallows dive under the bridge and swoop up on the other side, feeding on the flies and insects from the marsh.

Across the bridge, you continue on a boardwalk crossing over the dunes. Since this is a high-use area, the dunes are surrounded by fencing to protect the spartina and cordgrass. The grasses help anchor the coastal dunes, which protect the river zone behind them.

Turn right at 0.2 mile onto the wide, flat barrier beach. Walking toward the mouth of the Ogunquit River and with the dunes on your right, you will see more fencing and a sign posted. This enclosure is for nesting terns and piping plovers whose habitats are being destroyed gradually by coastal development. Piping plovers are inconspicuous sand-colored birds that blend in with the seascape, especially when snuggled into their bowl-like nests. If you don't see any plovers, you might hear their high piping call.

At 0.5 mile, another boardwalk bridge arcs back over the dunes. Turn away from the ocean and walk the boardwalk bridge over the grasses and beach roses. A few hardy pitch pines have also taken hold here.

When you get to the mud flats of the river, turn right and loop back toward the first footbridge. Sand near the dune fence makes walking difficult, but near the riverbed the nutrient-rich soil compacted with shells and marsh effluvia makes for more solid footing. Low tide spreads a table of delicacies for waders and other water birds.

Black-and-white least terns and sand-colored plovers (more difficult to spot) are increasing because of protection.

In the Ogonquit River's bed, bubbles emerging from the mud are a sure indication that Atlantic surf clams are buried in the intertidal ooze. These thick-shelled clams siphon water in and out through their tube-like feet. Along here, too, we were surprised to see a killdeer, which is at home in meadows and marsh grass. The killdeer looks like a plover but is twice as large, and in addition to the plover's neck ring, it wears a black bow tie.

This shore walk gives you an opportunity to bird

watch, especially if the tide is turning during evening hours. We identified a pair of greenish-legged pigeon-shaped upland sandpipers, which are occasionally found in grassy riverbank areas and tidal flats.

When you come in sight of the footbridge at 0.8 mile, look for a pass-through gate, allowing you to climb up from the riverbank and onto the bridge, and return to the parking area.

Ogunquit is a Natick Indian term meaning "beautiful place by the sea"—certainly a fitting description.

Jetty Walk
Wells Harbor
Wells, Maine

Distance: **1.2 miles**
Type of walk: **Out-and-back**
Approximate time: **30 minutes**
Difficulty: **Moderate**

*Visit a wide seawall for a broad perspective of the
Wells Harbor channel, Wells Beach and Drakes Island,
and a boardwalk through fragile dune habitat.*

Getting There

From the traffic light at the junction of US 1 and Mile Road in
Wells, drive east on Mile Road, which bisects a salt marsh feeding into the Webhannet River. In 1.2 miles, turn at the second
left onto Atlantic Avenue. Drive another 1.2 miles straight
into the Wells Harbor parking lot.

Special Features

- Boardwalk over sand dunes
- Wide pink granite jetty extending into the ocean
- Harbor views
- Shorebirds and harbor seals

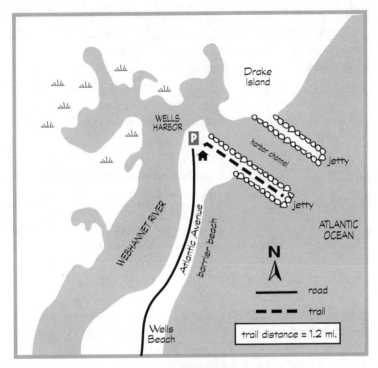

Jetty Walk

A breakwater is a barrier designed to protect a harbor or beach from the force of ocean waves. The jetty boulders at Wells Harbor are flat sided and secure for safe walking (when the waves aren't crashing over the breakwater). However, pay careful attention to the gaps between the boulders and take deliberate steps. The channel directs boats behind the Wells barrier beach to the mouth of the Webhannet River.

The trail begins at the information board located in the large parking area overlooking Wells Harbor. The board informs visitors about beach dune protection and the conservation efforts for the piping plover and least tern, two rare birds along the Maine coast.

To walk out along the west side of the harbor mouth and granite breakwater, you can choose either to walk on the boardwalk over the dunes, which parallels the jetty to the immediate right (facing the ocean), or begin on top of the breakwater on the left. This is one of two granite jetties located at the mouth of the Webhannet River, protecting both beach and harbor from the powerful waves that roll in off the open Atlantic. The pink granite blocks of the jetty were quarried nearby at Bald Hills in Wells, which also supplied pink granite for the Tomb of the Unknown Soldier in Arlington, Virginia.

The boardwalk to the right of the jetty offers a habitat of American beach grass, wildflowers, and beach roses. A 250-yard boardwalk is laid on the right of the sand not only for easier walking, but also to protect the dune grasses and nesting terns and plovers. Choose either the boardwalk or jetty.

At 0.6 mile, fencing and signs to the right identify nesting areas of these two endangered birds. Wire fence enclosures—or, more properly, "exclosures"—are placed around the piping plover nests to keep out predators and human disturbances. Least terns are more likely to skydive toward intruders to drive them away from the nesting colonies.

At the end of the boardwalk, beach grass in low and sandy fields appears on the right of the path. The wide, long, flat beach stops about halfway on the walk out along the jetty. This could be a good place for younger children to stop walking the jetty and climb down to beach.

From here, the breakwater extends beyond the beach into the Atlantic, and the footing becomes more uneven—the jetty blocks are not quite as flat and tightly fitted together as at the outset.

If you walk out along the jetty breakwater beyond the shoreline, the vista stretches to Wells Beach to the south. Walking high on the breakwater adds to the sweep of the scene. Kennebunkport is visible to the north. Closer up, lobster buoys bob in the water. Across the channel, bordered by a parallel jetty, is the residential area of Drakes Island.

At 0.6 mile, a green sign with a green light lines up with a red light and red sign on the other side of the breakwater channel, directing boats in and out of the harbor. In nautical terms, these lights are called lateral markers. They're positioned according to the so-called three R rule, "Red right returning": the red light is always positioned on the right (starboard) side on return from the sea; the green light is on the left (port) side.

The boat channel is also a flyway into the harbor and Webhannet marsh, behind the Wells barrier beach, for sea ducks (small and black)

The pink granite in this jetty was quarried at Wells.

and cormorants (larger and black), both of which are long necked and good divers.

On your return to the parking area, the protected side of the harbor at the public landing offers children a chance to fish for pollack, mackerel, small stripers, flounder, and small crabs at high tide.

Little River and Barrier Beach Walk

Trip 40 **Wells National Estuarine Research Reserve at Laudholm Farm (1,600 acres)**

Wells, Maine

Distance: **2.5 miles**
Type of walk: **Figure-eight Loop**
Approximate time: **1½ hours**
Difficulty: **Moderate**

A walk around the meadows and forest of a former upland farm, with overviews of rich and diverse tidal habitats along the Little River estuary and Laudholm Barrier Beach.

Getting There

From the intersections of US 1 with ME 9/109 at the traffic light in Wells, drive north on US 1 for 0.6 mile. Turn right onto Laudholm Farm Road and drive 1.4 miles. Turn left onto Skinner Mill Road, drive 0.2 mile, and turn right onto the Laudholm Farm Reserve access road. Drive 0.3 mile to the reserve entrance and parking lot.

Special Features

- A total of 7 miles of trails
- Meadows, woodlands, estuary, and barrier beach overlooks
- Visitor center, gift shop, research station
- Many educational activities, exhibits, and special events

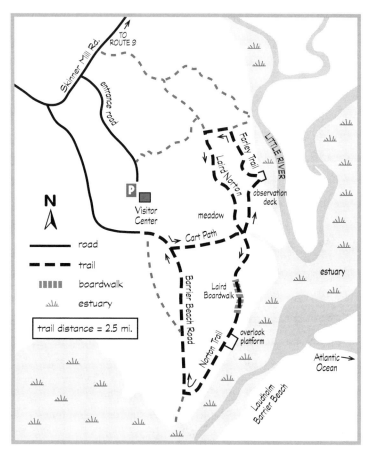

Little River and Barrier Beach Walk

The Wells National Estuarine Research Reserve at Laudholm Farm is not only a paradisiacal place to walk along the Little River estuary, but it is also vastly important in the overall health and vitality of the northern New England coast.

The reserve is one of twenty-five national estuarine research reserves managed by the National Oceanic and Atmospheric Administration (NOAA). Situated in a prime seacoast location in southern Maine, the 1,600-acre reserve includes parts of two watersheds—the Little River estuary and an eastern arm of the Webhannet River. The reserve is comprised of many interacting ecological zones, including a salt marsh (1 acre produces 10 tons of organic material), barrier beach, upland meadow, and forest.

Little River may indeed be little, but in conjunction with Branch Brook and Merriland River the watershed reaches from Sanford and the Kennebunks to Wells. This watershed is comparatively undeveloped, yet pollutants from lawns, roads, septic systems, and rain runoff from parking lots are slowly impacting the water quality and riparian ecosystem. Research studies indicate that 70 percent of the fish caught off the Atlantic seaboard depend for survival on estuaries like this one.

Formed in 1982, the Laudholm Trust's mission is to conserve and educate. One outgrowth of the Laudholm Trust's conservation efforts has been the Coastal Mosaic Project, which targets threats to the ecosystem (such as a 1,000-acre subdivision and golf course) and is working toward a comprehensive Little River Watershed Plan.

A new visitor center with interactive exhibits has been built, and you may want to stop in before or after your walk. A scrapbook with photos of flora and fauna in the estuary reserve is useful for identifying plants you may have seen.

The reserve's four major trails cover 7 miles. This walk combines loops on two trails—the Farley and Laird-Norton Trails—and takes in many prominent features of the Little River estuary.

The main trailhead is just east of the visitor center, where an impressive copper beech tree near the gazebo marks the path to the signpost for all trails. This ornamental member of the Beech family has handsome foliage and in fall produces nuts within triangular burs.

Beginning on the Cart Path, you soon reach a fork where Knights Trail and Barrier Beach Road branch right. Stay on the Cart Path, veering left along a fenced-in pasture. As you walk, imagine this large farm with its teams of horses and oxen bringing in the high mowings of upland meadow grass and tidal salt hay and carting apples from the orchard. To the right is a tall forest of maples.

At 0.4 mile, the Cart Path is gated. Turn left (at the sign) onto Farley Trail, passing edge forest on the right and open fields to the left. The forest provides habitat for foxes, white-tailed deer, owls, and hawks—all of which forage in the meadow.

At 0.5 mile, you come to a boardwalk into the forest. The boardwalk not only protects delicate wildflowers and insects of the forest floor but also keeps ticks from crawling up your legs. Since deer live in the reserve and deer ticks carry Lyme disease, it's a good idea to pull up your socks and keep to the paths.

At the edge of the evergreen forest of hemlocks and spruce is an observation deck overlooking Little River. Here we saw firsthand some of the reserve's educational outreach exhibits set up on the observation deck, including a tank with several fish species common to Little River. Minuscule sticklebacks are categorized as three-spine, four-spine, or nine-spine. Because four-spines have the most salinity tolerance, you're more apt to find them in areas with salt pannes—standing saltwater ponds created by unusually high tides such as those during the spring full moon. Mummichogs are nearly the same size, brown, and have vertical silver bands. Pipefish, which look like flattened sea horses, are related to the mummichogs and are also quite small. Mom pipefish lays her eggs in Dad's brood pouch. Atlantic silversides feed on fish larvae and insects. When they're fingerling size, they migrate to sea.

Most interesting are the American eels. Young glass eels, or elvers, are carried by the Gulf Stream into tidal estuaries like this. Eels grow (male eels grow to two feet in length, females to four feet) in length, and they can live to eighteen years. All eels return to the Sargasso Sea, located south of Bermuda, where they mate and spawn in the tropical brown sargassum seaweed, and then new elvers start their travels north via the Gulf Stream.

Twice a day tidal waters in the marsh sweep away debris, cleaning and filtering the water. Plankton produce half the oxygen in the world, an invaluable part of the cleansing process. The marsh sits on millennia-old peat dense and rich in nutrients. To give an idea how all of these factors work together, consider that a 1,500-acre tidal marsh (about the size of this estuary) is capable of naturally purifying the wastewater from a city of 60,000 people.

From the observation deck at 0.65 mile, retrace your steps and continue on the dirt trail, with the river on your right. Watch your step—pine roots often surface on the trail.

Ascend to a thicket of bushes interspersed with old apple trees. This area slowly is changing from the farmland it once was to the forest you just left. The "early successional habitat" of shrubs provides a perfect cover for the New England cottontail. These light-brown bunnies, growing to weigh 2 pounds as adults, are well camouflaged in their own network of trails through the undergrowth.

Several large, old sugar maples line the trail. One old maple has turned into a "snag," its dead trunk a host to plate-size shelf mushrooms. In addition to nurturing fungi, snags provide shelter for animals and birds in the tunnels and crevices of their standing trunks.

At 0.8 mile, the path becomes a grassy swath and winds through a stand of birches and a small clearing. Then once again you're walking on pine needles and stepping over white pine roots.

At 0.9 mile you reach a T junction. At this point, you have walked half of Farley Trail. Turn left onto Laird-Norton Trail.

At 1.0 mile, you reach a wondrously large meadow surrounded by a thick forest of deciduous trees and white pines. Skirting the forest periphery to the left, you'll soon come to a large "pasture pine": when farm cattle and sheep browse on young white pine branches, the result is a pine with several trunks. Follow the mowed swath through a "high mowing," an area of grassy upland pasture mowed by farmers for hay. In the distance, on the right, are the barns and outbuildings of Laudholm Farm; on the left is Little River marsh where farmers piled salt hay atop circular staddles (wooden posts) to dry for winter fodder.

Meadows attract a variety of wildlife, including flickers, meadowlarks, wrens, grasshoppers, and field mice. Wild red raspberry, ox-eye daisy, angelica, pearly everlasting, and bright yellow yarrow dot the field throughout the summer.

The grassy path loops back to the Cart Path intersection (gated area) at 1.3 miles.

Cross the Cart Path and follow the sign to Laird-Norton Trail through the forest of tall, second-growth maples. This area seems to attract birds. We spotted a yellow-rumped

Skunk cabbage in a marshy peat bog near Little River.

warbler in the maple leaf canopy, and a rufous-sided towhee flew down to greet us with its distinctive loud *tooo-hee* call.

A boardwalk protects wildflowers on the damp forest floor. Hay-scented ferns, cinnamon ferns, and tall royal ferns proliferate among the pipsissewa and magenta orchidlike flowers of fringed polygala (gaywings).

At 1.4 miles, you come to a boggy area. Water-loving blue flags (wild irises) and skunk cabbage thrive in this marshy peat bog. The boardwalk connects with a deck overlooking a strand of white sand, the Laudholm Barrier Beach, on the Atlantic Ocean. Many barrier beaches like this exist along the north Atlantic seaboard. Each is associated with a rocky headland impacted by waves. Water circulates around the headland and river inlets—in this case Little River and the tidal marsh.

Extending beyond the observation deck is the vast marsh and a meander of Little River.

During the last ice age (from 7,000 to 9,000 years ago), a receding glacier left an inland sea and glacial lakes, dumping and crushing rocks, compressing decayed matter into peat beds, and decimating cedar forests that once grew out to the barrier beach. The sea rose as the glacier melted, then slowed to 2 millimeters per year. Global warming has produced a 2-degree temperature rise, and it's possible that in another century this observation deck could be under the ocean. The Wells Reserve and Maine Coastal Program have published and reprinted a popular booklet, *The Sea Is Rising,* available at the visitor center.

Continue on the boardwalk, walking through a mixed forest of golden birches (easily identified by their shiny gold-colored bark) and clumps of red "swamp" maples whose leaves are the first to turn crimson in fall.

At 1.8 miles, you come to a research study area marked by a wire fence "exclosure." Red maple, white birch, and red oak are penned in, and the overabundant white-tailed deer and invasive Japanese barberry plants kept out. Japanese bayberry was introduced into America in the 1800s. It was favored as a thorny hedge to discourage predators from entering chicken coops, vegetable gardens, and houses. We have occasionally seen a few barberry bushes in overgrown forest areas near cellar holes. But at the reserve, barberry grows nearly everywhere; if it's left unchecked, many other species won't survive. At 2.0 miles, the Laird-Norton Trail intersects Barrier Beach Road. You can hear the surf on Laudholm Beach to the left and continue your walk there if you wish. Turn right onto Beach Road and walk 0.5 mile to the copper beech and visitor center.

Hours, Fees, and Facilities

The gift shop in the visitor center has identification booklets for children, and reservations are taken for "Just for Kids" half-day programs and events throughout the summer. The busy schedule of summer activities for all ages includes sky watches, night walks, geology, and wildflower tours.

For More Information

Laudholm Farm, P.O. Box 1007, Wells, ME 04090; 207-646-1555; www.laudholm.org.

Knight Trail

Wells National Estuarine Research Reserve at Laudholm Farm (1,600 acres)

Wells, Maine

Distance: **0.6 mile**
Type of walk: **Loop**
Approximate time: **45 minutes**
Difficulty: **Easy**

*A short, sweet loop through a hilltop fruit orchard and high
mowing overlooking the grand estuary of the Webhannet River.*

Getting There

From the intersection of US 1 with ME 9/109 at the traffic light
in Wells, drive north on US 1 for 0.6 mile. Turn right onto
Laudholm Farm Road and drive 1.4 miles. Turn left onto Skinner Mill Road, drive 0.2 mile, and turn right onto the Laudholm Farm Reserve access road. Drive 0.3 mile to the reserve
entrance and parking lot.

Special Features

• Orchard blossoms in spring
• Overlook of Webhannet estuary
• Visitor center with exhibits and programs

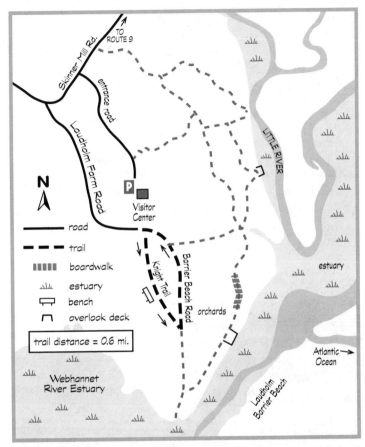

Knight Trail

The Knight Trail offers many pleasant views of the surrounding countryside and is one of the shorter trails in the reserve.

Laudholm Farm is one of twenty-five national estuarine research reserves managed by the National Oceanic and

Atmospheric Administration (NOAA). Situated in a prime seacoast location, the reserve includes parts of the Little River and Webhannet River watersheds as they flow into the Atlantic Ocean. Several ecological areas, including a salt marsh, barrier beach, upland meadows, and forest make up the reserve. Research studies indicate that 70 percent of the fish caught off the Atlantic seaboard depend for survival on estuaries like this one.

From the Laudholm Farm Visitor Center, walk to the main trailhead at the giant copper beech tree where the Knight Trail begins, heading south. Follow the mowed-grass trail across the open meadow of this former upland farm.

In about 200 yards, you'll reach some benches overlooking the Webhannet River valley below and an untouched rural area of Wells. In spring and early summer apple trees of the old orchard are in bloom, birds sing constantly, and meadow wildflowers thrive.

This overgrown orchard at Laudholm Farm attracts a variety of birds.

The birdhouses scattered about this area have galvanized steel cones designed to keep squirrels and other predators from marauding the nests. Catbirds and chokecherry trees, too, live in this high mowing where birdsong and distant sea sounds intermingle. Swallows swoop in and out of the orchard, and goldfinches bob through the foliage.

Knight Trail is wide and accommodating, passing through shrubbery and brush areas. Notice the widespread barberry plants, once used as hedges around farm buildings. The thorns are everywhere on this tangly bush; in fact, the apple orchard is overgrown by this resilient plant. Japanese barberry was introduced to America in the 1800s. It was favored as a thorny hedge to discourage predators from chicken coops, vegetable gardens, and houses, but time has shown that it tends to compete with other plants and take over. Many of this book's walks encounter barberries, and we have occasionally seen a few barberry bushes in overgrown forest areas near old cellar holes. But at the reserve, barberry grows nearly everywhere; many other native species won't survive here unless this aggressive plant is checked. Fortunately, efforts are under way to eradicate it, thanks to a unique partnership between Laudholm and a local business.

After a short downhill section, the trail forks at 0.25 mile (the halfway point). Make a sharp left onto Barrier Beach Road and head north across the brushy meadow to a Y junction. Bear left onto Cart Path and pass a stone wall on the left. Continue back to the trailhead, passing a lilac hedge on the right.

For More Information
Laudholm Farm, P.O. Box 1007, Wells, ME 04090; 207-646-1555; www.laudholm.org.

Carson Trail

Rachel Carson National Wildlife Refuge (44 acres)

Wells, Maine

Distance: 1.0 mile
Type of walk: Loop
Approximate time: 30–45 minutes
Difficulty: Easy

A well-designed, wide footpath through prime edge
tidal habitats at the confluence of Little River,
Branch Brook, and Merriland River.

Getting There

From the junction of US 1 and ME 9 in Wells at Cozy Corners, turn onto ME 9 east and drive 0.7 mile toward Kennebunkport to the Rachel Carson National Wildlife Refuge sign and parking lot on the right.

Special Features

• Identification trail with stations
• Decks overlooking salt marshes
• Universal accessibility with hard pack trails

Rachel Carson (1907–64), the world-renowned aquatic biologist and author of *Silent Spring* and *The Sea Around Us*, was a

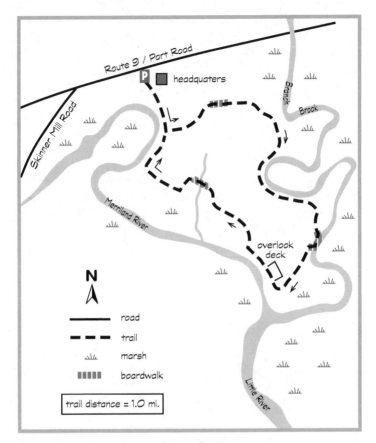

Carson Trail

remarkable woman. Her research and writings not only altered widespread use of pesticides in the United States but also laid the foundation for global conservation efforts. "All the life of the planet is interrelated," she wrote. "Each species has its own ties to others, and all are related to the earth."

The ten Rachel Carson National Wildlife Refuge areas in Maine extend intermittently from Kittery on the Piscataqua River to Cape Elizabeth near Scarborough. The refuge parcels total 7,435 acres and include 50 miles of coastline. They are vital to preserving and ensuring habitat for waterfowl and migrating birds. More than 250 species have been sighted. Although the refuge is vast, this is the only parcel with public access on the refuge flyway.

This self-guided tour provides a basic introduction to the coastal environment and what you might see in a north Atlantic estuary. Before starting the walk, stop by the visitor center to pick up a map and informative brochure highlighting some of the programs and sights.

The first overlook (Station 1) shows a tidal meander (a winding river), and if you look closely you can see what convenient homesites the undercut riverbank provides for otter and other animals. You stand in an upland edge with the river below and tidal marsh beyond. All these zones are vital to the health of the coast. When trees and meadows are bulldozed for houses, the marsh habitat is filled and eventually disappears.

Each month throughout spring and summer, different wildflowers bloom (Station 2). In May the flowering bridal bush holds its lacy white bouquets against the tall dark trunks of white pines (five-needled bunches), while the orchidlike magenta fringed polygala (gaywings) pushes up through the hemlock needles.

At Station 3, you reach an observation deck overlooking Branch Brook. Twice a day Little River acts as a conduit for the tides, which are channeled into Branch Brook on one side of this peninsula of land, and Merriland River on the other.

Dedication Trail at Rachel Carson Refuge is one of 10 tidal preserves.

As the tides dig deeper channels (Station 4), riverbanks slump and soil washes to other parts of the marsh. Decayed flora at the forest edge is also swept away by high spring tides (at the new and full moons).

Salt pannes (Station 5) are like marsh tide pools. As the tide falls, the water is trapped in these low areas, often circular in shape. The warmth and fecundity of the water breeds invertebrates in these pantries for waterfowl. A high concentration of salt is left behind when the brackish water evaporates. Only sea-blite, glasswort, and other specialized salt-tolerant plants can survive in such environments.

At Station 6, saltwater and salt meadow spartina cordgrass is the dominant species. Coastal farmers used to depend on high-marsh hay fields for winter fodder for their animals. Marsh hay is abundant and is still used by farmers. The yield of 1 acre of marsh hay is the equivalent of a megafarm in the Midwest.

A bench at Station 7 offers a magnificent view Branch Brook merging into Little River leading to the Atlantic Ocean. This active flux of waters creates a diverse and rich bounty of insects, sea worms, shellfish, and clams as well as feeding waterfowl.

Stations 10 and 11 demonstrate the importance of buffer zones between human and wildlife habitats. In a ravine below the trail, Merriland River fills with snowmelt in spring but may dry up during summer. Though the stream is intermittent, it plays a vital role in the delicate balance of nature, providing fresh water for white-tailed deer, songbirds, and other inhabitants of the refuge.

The trail ends here. However, visitors to the refuge can take with them what they have learned about coastal areas.

For More Information

Rachel Carson National Wildlife Refuge, 321 Port Road, Building A, Wells, ME 04090; 207-546-9226.

Plains Pond Trail

Kennebunk Blueberry Plains (1,100 acres)

Kennebunk, Maine

Distance: **0.6 mile**
Type of walk: **Loop**
Approximate time: **30 minutes**
Difficulty: **Easy**

A sandy plain located over a large aquifer bubbling into a small pond bordered by woods and grasses.

Getting There

From US 1 in the center of Kennebunk, turn west onto ME 9A. At 0.2 mile, turn right (west) onto ME 99 and drive 4.5 miles. ME 99 will cross I-95 and bear left at a fork to the Kennebunk Plains parking corral on the right (north) side of the road. Pull into the lot and read the information signboard; then drive or walk across ME 99 to the access road and parking corral on the other (south) side.

Special Features

- Freshwater pond and rare birds
- Tussock grasses
- Heath blooms and berries

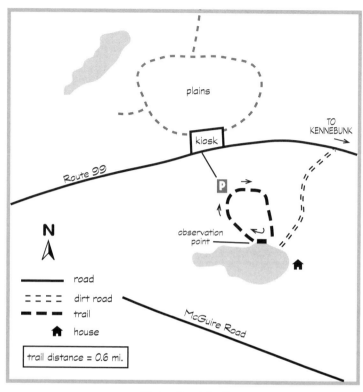

Plains Pond Trail

Take the sand road to the right of the corral heading away from ME 99. Ongoing research and revitalization of certain areas may prevent access to roads, but an alternative route will be indicated. In summer a variety of grasses grow together in close-knit "bunches," or tussocks, to provide a collective network of shoots and roots that more efficiently retain moisture.

Stop to examine the shrubs of the Heath family (Ericaceae), which include lowbush and highbush blueberry, bearberry, and huckleberry. In the woodier areas, sheep laurel and the larger heath shrubs proliferate. Heaths are survivors equipped to endure droughtlike conditions and periodic burnings for blueberry growth on these windswept plains. Their roots enjoy a symbiotic relationship with fungus (mycorrhizae) that allows them to extract nitrogen and other nutrients from the soil. The slender, leathery leaves of the heaths protect the plant from harsh wind and sun yet funnel morning dewdrops to their roots. In spring, bearberry and other flowering heaths collect rain in white and pink bell-shaped blossoms.

During hot summers when the sand plain blazes like a desert, their reddish stems, branches, and leaves admit the red spectrum of sunlight, filtering out more destructive rays.

At 0.2 mile, the rutted sand road leads toward a private house on a small pond and dam. Beneath the Kennebunk Plains lies a 70-foot leach field of gravel and sand deposited by a glacier 12,000 years ago. Another glacial legacy is the huge aquifer, which supplies

Wildflowers include endangered species of northern blazing star and commoner field flowers.

many towns in the area with drinking water. The dam and house at the east end of the pond are located on private property and are off-limits. However, the other three sides of the wooded pond make the open shore an ideal birding spot.

Birds nesting on the plain frequent this pool. They include grasshopper sparrows, upland sandpipers, horned larks, and vesper sparrows—all endangered as their habitat diminishes due to coastal development. At the pond's edge, chances are better that you'll see the more common species like the catbird we heard practicing its trills and arpeggios at the wooded water's edge. A flicker swooped in from the field. One of the larger woodpeckers, the flicker is identified by a bright-red nape, black neckerchief, large tawny-brown body, white flashy rump, and a preference for periphery wood-and-meadow habitats such as this.

When you turn away from the pond, you're facing a junction where the road you came in on meets a wide sand road leading to ME 99 and a smaller path looping 0.2 mile back to the parking corral, in view. Take the smaller path (unless it's blocked by a research sign, in which case you must retrace your steps).

Coyotes are often spotted in this area. On our way back, we spotted one that might have been to the reservoir for a drink of cool fresh water and circled back to spy on us. We also spotted hunters' cartridge shells, mountain bike tire ruts, and plants uprooted by horse hooves. Many of the plant species that grow here are endangered. Please use care to stay on the marked paths.

Sand Plains Trail

Kennebunk Blueberry Plains (1,100 acres)

Kennebunk, Maine

Distance: 1.0 mile
Type of walk: Loop
Approximate time: 30 minutes
Difficulty: Easy

A large, open field with lowbush blueberries and other groundcover plants, the rare grasshopper sparrow, the world's largest population of the rare northern blazing star, and uncommon wildflowers and grasses.

Getting There

From US 1 in the center of Kennebunk, turn west onto ME 9A. At 0.2 mile, turn right (west) onto ME 99 and drive 4.5 miles. ME 99 will cross I-95 and bears left at a fork to the Kennebunk Plains parking corral on the right (north) side of the road.

Special Features
• Open-field walking
• Blueberry picking in midsummer
• Bunchgrasses and wildflowers

From reading the large signboard at the parking corral, you'll learn that this coastal sand plain and grassland provides critical

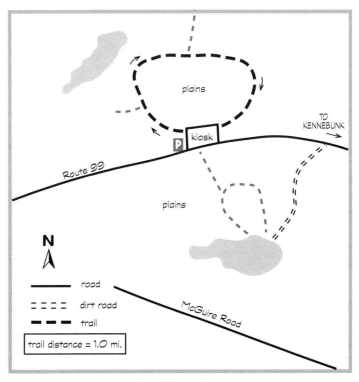

Sand Plains Trail

habitats for several threatened and endangered species. These coastal plains are characterized by native "bunching" grasses. Rains percolate through sand, and the grasses bunch together to hold the moisture in a solidarity of shoots and roots under the hot summer sun.

This short sand plains loop, shaped like a racing track, gives visitors wide-open spaces bordering a forest of scrub oak, aspen, and gray birch.

Facing the huge signboard at the parking corral, take the sandy road that circles clockwise. In about 20 yards, another sand road comes in from the left; keep to the right.

Many shrubs in the large tract belong to the Heath family, including chokeberry, bearberry, and blueberry. In July the plains turn blue with one of Maine's most popular—and important—crops. Statewide, Maine produces 99 percent of all blueberries grown in the country.

Because berries thrive in the wake of fire, The Nature Conservancy—in conjunction with the Maine Department of Inland Fisheries and Wildlife—supervises controlled burns on the plains, with the help of volunteer crews and a fire specialist, to burn away decayed vegetation and revitalize plant growth. The burns also revitalize the habitat for turkey, deer, foxes, and other creatures. You'll probably see a few ash-darkened spots scattered here and there. Native Americans and early settlers in the area also set fires to renew their sources of berries and plants.

Before the use of controlled fires, blueberry management unfortunately consisted of spraying herbicides. This maintained the blueberries but killed many

Kennebunk Plains is host to bearberries, blackberries, chokeberries, and other members of the Heath family.

other plant species. Now in early spring, although burned roots look rather desolate, new green bunchgrasses and wildflowers proliferate.

On our walk in April, a grasshopper sparrow that resides in the plains followed us along the road. The grasshopper sparrow is in decline across the United States because the prairie and field grasslands habitats are disappearing to development. Grasshopper sparrows are 4$\frac{1}{2}$ inches long, and have bright-yellow shoulders, short sharp tails, and unmarked breasts. They zigzag through shrubs and hop through the bunchgrasses.

In spring, walking toward the back side of the loop at 0.4 mile, we saw a lone coyote trotting in the distance. As we approached, the wary canine spotted us, too, and disappeared into the sparse undercover of flowering bearberries and aspen saplings.

Each month brings a new color palette and aspect to these plains. In July it's difficult to walk here without stopping every few feet to roll a handful of ripe blueberries into your mouth.

In August, the plains turn a vibrant magenta with the blooms of northern blazing stars. One of several endangered species that thrive here, these tall field flowers with narrow leaves are thought to be the largest remaining population in the world. Plumelike in appearance, their composite flowers around a central quill-like stem have led to the nickname gay-feathers. Other rare plant species include toothed white-topped aster (found at only one other site in Maine) and upright bindweed.

At 0.75 mile, a path forks off to the left and, shortly after, another path connects from the left. Continue circling to the right on the open plain back to the trailhead.

Mousam River Oxbow Trail
Kennebunk Bridle Path
Kennebunk, Maine

Distance: **0.75 mile**
Type of walk: **Out-and-back**
Approximate time: **30 minutes**
Difficulty: **Easy**

*An abandoned railroad bed and a short side trail leading
to the broad, grassy banks of the Mousam River.*

Getting There
From the junction of Summer Street and Portland Road (US 1)
at the Central Fire Station in downtown Kennebunk, drive 0.6
mile on Summer Street (ME 35). Turn right onto Sea Road and
drive 0.7 mile past Sea Road School on the right. Turn right
onto Mere Street and drive 0.25 mile to a parking area with a
utility maintenance box on the left next to the Bridle Path.

Special Features
- A prime river oxbow
- Turtles and herons
- Estuarial grassy land plateau
- Part of 3-mile-long Bridle Path

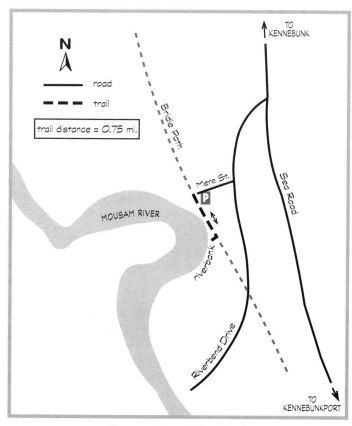

Mousam River Oxbow Trail

The Bridle Path, a total of 3 miles long, begins at the depot in Kennebunk, parallels a meandering section of the Mousam River (this walk), and sweeps around the east side of the river mouth to end at Sea Road a few blocks from the Atlantic

Ocean (see walk 46). Some parts of the path are in a residential area, but the views here along the river still evoke the wild and the wonderful. Landowners along the pathway vary from public to private and include the U.S. Fish and Wildlife Department, the Kennebunk Land Trust, and the Kennebunk Water and Sewage Department. Although some sections are privately owned, public access is allowed along the Bridle Path. Please remember to stay on the trail and respect the rights of the property owners as you pass by.

The trail begins at the parking area. Enjoy the easy stroll through the open woods along a wide, straight section of trail that follows an abandoned railroad bed. This section of the Bridle Path hides nearby homes fairly well until 200 yards into the walk, where the last house appears through the thick woods on the right.

As you walk along the multiuse trail, you'll catch glimpses of the Mousam River on your right through the woods. The common bracken ferns (also called brake-fern) are plentiful here, as they are throughout the world. The coarse texture of the fronds, unlike other triangular ferns, is one of their identifying features.

At 0.2 mile on the right, look for the side trail. Walk down this narrow trail, and in less than another 0.1 mile the vista opens directly onto the Mousam River. This lush scene of the river winding in broad sweeps through the high, dry, grassy embankments makes a breathtaking sight. A river oxbow (like the shape of the bows on an ox yoke) is a wide U-shaped bend in a river. This particular example clearly shows how the unrelenting force of a river can alter a riverscape. In time, the river will break through the land neck and the river will straighten out its line of direction.

A footbridge leads to an oxbow of Mousam River.

From the shore, you can see how the grassy, earth-packed peninsula falls away through constant erosion, especially where the river current hits hard. Large slabs of bottomland along the bank slip and wash away into the river.

A two-plank, 8-foot-long footbridge takes you from the shore onto the broad oxbow neck where you can see the erosion up close. Stay close to the footbridge and look for crickets, frogs, and mud turtles. Turtles lay their eggs on land, so be careful not to step on turtle nests. Return by the same route.

Mousam River Estuary Trail

Kennebunk Bridle Path

Kennebunkport, Maine

Trip 46

Distance: **1.5 miles**
Type of walk: **Out-and-back**
Approximate time: **1 hour**
Difficulty: **Easy**

*An old railroad bed through an open salt marsh with long
views to the Atlantic before entering rich woodlands.*

Getting There

From Dock Square in downtown Kennebunkport, drive 2.1
miles west on ME 9. Immediately before a bridge over the
Mousam River, a break in the woods identifies the Bridle Path.
Park at the turnoff on the right side of ME 9. Cross ME 9 (care-
fully) to the trailhead for this walk.

Special Features

- Unobstructed views of Mousam River estuary
- Popular, level, multiuse trail
- Part of the 3-mile-long Bridle Path

This walk is part of the Bridle Path, a 3-mile multiuse trail that
begins in downtown Kennebunk and follows an old railroad

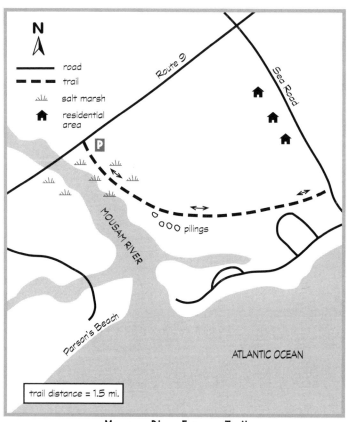

N

road
trail
salt marsh
residential area

P

Route 9

Sea Road

MOUSAM RIVER

pilings

Parson's Beach

ATLANTIC OCEAN

trail distance = 1.5 mi.

Mousam River Estuary Trail

bed boardering the meandering Mousam River (see walk 45), a tidal estuary. This final section of the pathway includes a salt marsh that extends to the ocean, with views of the sand dunes in the distance. The trail begins at a wide entrance on the ocean side of ME 9 but narrows right away.

About 70 yards into the walk, Mousam River can be seen to the right beyond the marsh and backwater tidal ditches. The narrow trail on the raised levee is bordered by scrub oak and Scotch pine saplings. On this pleasant isthmus through the backwaters of the Mousam estuary, you see a good example of how a barrier beach forms: strong tides at the mouth of the river have chiseled backwater channels that eventually become open water of the tidal river. Sand dunes on the other side of the river at Parsons Beach also are forming a barrier.

In another 70 yards on the pine-needle path, boundary signs on the left identify this as Mousam River division of the Rachel Carson National Wildlife Refuge, which is comprised of about 7,435 acres (see walk 42). The trail is maintained by Kennebunk Land Trust and other organizations.

Watch for bearberry, a low, evergreen shrub with thick, oval leaves and waxy white flowers in spring, followed by smooth, red, pea-size berries in late summer and fall. Bears like bearberries, but you'll see no bears here. Instead, numerous white-winged scoter and mallard ducks visit the right side of the trail where the marsh weaves through grass-topped mud banks.

This section of Bridle Trail borders a tidal estuary near Kennebunkport.

The path opens up and then dead-ends at the old railroad pilings. Just walk left, down, and around to get back on the trail. Continue along a profuse hedge of pink and white beach roses (wild roses have fewer petals than most hybrid, cultivated roses).

Look for the purple blossoms of beach peas, especially in early summer. The path narrows again with brush and shrubs (lots of Japanese honeysuckle). Catbirds, chickadees, and red-winged blackbirds abound along here.

At 0.3 mile, forest margin acts as a buffer zone near residential property. A sign to the right reads: "This area is a sanctuary of the Kennebunk Land Trust—for scientific and educational use." This parcel is known as the Madelyn Marx Preserve. In this more inland area, interrupted ferns, bracken ferns, and mayflowers are groundcover in a mixed fir and spruce forest. Close to the right side of the trail, we saw a fine lady's slipper, the rose-colored wild orchid, in bloom in May. These are obscure wildflowers, but once you see them they're readily identified by the hanging pouch and leaf-stem curled over the bloom. At 0.6 mile, exposed tree roots can be slippery when damp. The ambience is completely different from the first half of the walk. The upland forest is more open, with sunlight filtering down through the tree branches to the edge-loving plants such as meadow rue and barberry. You might hear the high, clear notes of cardinals.

At 0.75 mile, the trail emerges onto Sea Road—a residential area. Return on the same path.

Once you're back at your car, you may want to drive down Sea Road from ME 9 to the end of the trail and then to Beach Avenue. Turn left and drive 0.2 mile to Mothers Beach, where a children's playground and parking are available.

Parsons Way Trail

Parsons Way

Kennebunkport, Maine

Trip 47

Distance: **2.0 miles**
Type of walk: **Out-and-back**
Approximate time: **1 hour**
Difficulty: **Easy**

A cliff walk around the bold shorefront of Cape Arundel to Spouting Rock and Blowing Cave, with dramatic views of the ocean.

Getting There

From Dock Square in Kennebunkport, drive east on Ocean Avenue for 1.3 miles. Parking is limited near the stone pillars at St. Ann's Church, where Parsons Way begins. Alternate parking is available at Colony Beach, a few hundred yards back on the right.

Special Features

- High surf and ocean spray
- Wave-carved blowholes
- Long coastline views

Parsons Way is named after Henry Parsons, who gave the land to Kennebunkport "so that everyone may enjoy its natural

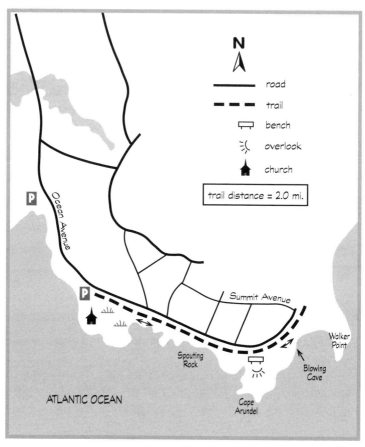

Parsons Way Trail

beauty." We've met a few power walkers on Parsons Way, but this is a walk meant for dallying, so you can savor the surf, the spouting sea clefts, and the ever-changing views as you round Cape Arundel.

Pitch pines shade the driveway to the handsome, stone St. Ann's Church, where this walk officially begins. These pines grow all along the northeastern seaboard and were once valuable for shipbuilding.

At the outset, Parsons Way is a sand path bordering a small cattail swamp, then becomes a sidewalk. This swampy area is surprisingly active for a popular byway. When we were last here in spring, male red-winged blackbirds sat on cattail stalks *trilling* and calling for mates. Meanwhile, several walkers with cameras took close-up family photos of a mother mallard and a flotilla of ducklings. Unruffled by the attention, the drake stood on a hollow log preening his iridescent green neck feathers.

Across Ocean Avenue, large Victorian summer cottages dominate the landscape, but on the ocean side, nature is left to fit in the nooks and crannies of seawalls and rocky coves. A tangle of beach alder, Japanese honeysuckle, and other hardy shrubs create a dense cover for songbirds and beach sparrows. A *word of warning:* Avoid stepping into overgrown areas unless a path is clearly marked. Poison ivy (three shiny leaves on reddish stems) is alive and thriving.

At 0.2 mile, stairs lead to a narrow pebble cove cut into chiseled granite slabs that channel the pounding seawater.

After negotiating a seawall at 0.3 mile, you'll come to another cove. At 0.4 mile is a bluff where booming surf sprays the ledges along the bluff. Locals have named it Spouting Rock. All along the shore, waves forced into rock caverns shoot geysers into the air, looking like a pod of spouting whales on their way along the coast.

At 0.5 mile, take a dirt path onto a grassy bluff. Benches have been placed on this idyllic spot for walkers to observe the dramatic surf. Beach roses proliferate on this open bluff.

Benches are located along the park shoreline of Parsons Way.

Redosier (a member of the Dogwood family) also thrives here as a shrub and is identified by its reddish stems.

Back on the avenue, at 0.6 mile, above a private garden, is the canopy of a large ornamental catalpa tree. The clusters of six oblate leaves in spring produce striking upright clusters of bright white and yellow flowers. In fall these turn to long, brown pods.

Staghorn sumac trees also have upright flower clusters that turn bright red in late summer and fall. Also known as lemonade trees, staghorn sumacs provide vitamin C nourishment for birds in winter long after the sumac leaves have turned brilliant red and fallen. (Poison sumac—which like poison ivy produces a poisonous oil—has downward greenish white flowers.)

At the top of a knoll, the George H. Walker Bush compound on Walker Point, a private peninsula, comes into view. Walk along another seawall to a many-trunked red maple that marks a graduated descent from the knoll. In this area if you listen closely you'll pick up the sound of Blowing Cave. The siphoning and soughing of water in the cave produces a distinct bass tone. Here you might like to take advantage of a bench placed high on the promontory above the cove. The black chain fence near a few roadside parking spaces marks the mile point.

Return on the same path.

Kennebunk River Trail

Saint Anthony Franciscan Monastery (60 acres)

Kennebunkport, Maine

Distance: **1.0 mile**
Type of walk: **Loop**
Approximate time: **45 minutes**
Difficulty: **Easy**

*Tranquil wooded estate (monastery) on the western
shore of the Kennebunk River with human-made
and natural shrines for contemplation.*

Getting There

From Dock Square in Kennebunkport, drive 0.2 mile west on
ME 9 to Beach Avenue (ME 35). At the signal, turn left and
drive 0.3 mile to the stone pillar entrance to Saint Anthony
Franciscan Monastery on the left (28 Beach Avenue). Enter the
estate (monastery) access road and turn left to the parking area.

Special Features

• Overlooks of Kennebunkport Harbor
• Lithuanian-designed shrines
• Statue to Kateri, a Mohawk saint
• Ornamental trees

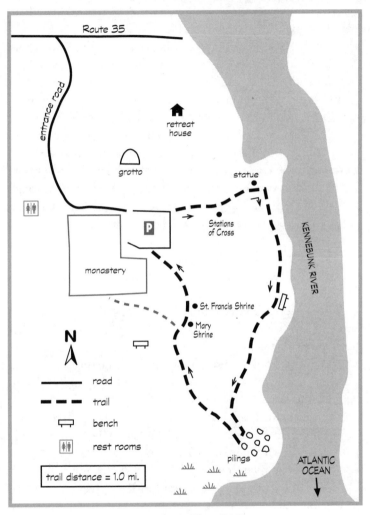

Kennebunk River Trail

Sir William Pepperrell, the famous military son of William Pepperrell of the Isles of Shoals and Kittery (see walk 30), claimed this land and sold 200 acres in 1740 to John Mitchell. Mitchell's ancestors lived on it until 1900, when an industrialist, William A. Rogers, built a Tudor-style mansion. After World War II, the land was purchased by Lithuanian Franciscans for a monastery; they have kindly opened it to the public.

Begin on an asphalt path located at the farthest corner of the parking lot. Walk to the triangular Lithuanian-designed Stations of the Cross enclosed by a wall. (A large retreat house is visible on your left across the lawn.) Curve right through azaleas and barberry shrubs—and flowering crab apples, too, in spring. You also walk past a pair of large white birches and a red oak.

At 0.2 mile, the path ascends a rocky outcrop topped by a statue of Kateri (Catherine) Tekakwivha. The inscription on the plaque reads, "Lily of the Mohawk Indians." Kateri was born in a Mohawk village in New York in 1656. She was baptized in 1676 and died in Canada in 1680. Pope Pius XII declared her "venerable" in 1943.

From this knoll and statue by the riverside, take a side trip (left) for a view of the busy harbor, boat traffic, and bridge in Kennebunkport.

Now keeping the river to your left, take the main footpath. At 0.4 mile, three benches are set in a semicircle. A narrow side path descends to tidal flats where you can see the grassy opposite bank of the river, town docks, and downtown buildings.

Continue walking the shore trail with the river on your left. In less than 200 yards at a Y junction, turn left near two mature white birches. Roots surface here, so watch your step. The winding river remains to the left.

At 0.5 mile, traverse two footbridges within 50 yards of each other. Wend your way through the woods to an open, grassy promontory with an unobstructed view of the Kennebunk River. This was once the site of a charming boathouse and pier. Unfortunately, the boathouse was vandalized and subsequently removed, with only the pilings remaining. This lovely spot is open to the public by the generosity of the Franciscans—please be respectful.

Turning away from the water, you'll soon come to a Y junction; bypass the trail you were on and veer left. Follow the pine-needle trail through an uncultivated area of woods back toward the monastery and chapel. The wide variety of trees and plant life here covers a full spectrum—from Japanese honeysuckle, beech trees, and barberry bushes to yellow birch, interrupted ferns, and wild apple trees.

When you come to a shrine with a statue of the Virgin Mary elevated on a rock garden, circle it and climb the steps. Continue on the asphalt trail and then pass through a forest of rhododendrons and white pines. You will come to a statue of Saint Francis playing a violin to a wolf and lamb. Throughout the forest, you can hear the sweet birdsong of cardinals, robins, orioles, and warblers.

Kateri Tekakwivha, "Lily of the Mohawk Indians."

At 0.75 mile, the final section of the trail takes you past ornamental plantings of Japanese red maple, a tall blue spruce, tree of heaven, mature magnolia, and ginkgo tree. The ginkgo has fan-shaped leaves, and its pungent, drooping yellow fruits are collected by squirrels in fall.

Hours, Fees, and Facilities
A gift shop has books and cards. Rest rooms are open during visiting hours.

For More Information
Saint Anthony Franciscan Monastery, P.O. Box 1980, Kennebunkport, ME 04046; 207-646-5115.

Vaughn Island Trail

Vaughn Island Preserve
(46 acres)

Kennebunkport, Maine

Distance: **0.75 mile**
Type of walk: **Loop**
Approximate time: **1 hour**
Difficulty: **Challenging**

*An island preserve between Porpoise Cove and Turbats Creek
connected at low tide to the mainland by a narrow tidal channel.*

Getting There

From Dock Square in Kennebunkport, drive 3.2 miles on
Ocean Avenue. Turn right at Turbats Creek Road and drive 0.2
mile to the end at Turbats Creek. A few parking places are
available across from the forested island.

Special Features

• Oak-forested island
• Low-tide discoveries
• Gulls, cormorants, sea ducks

Walking across Turbats Creek at low tide to Vaughn Island is an
adventure. A few people from Kennebunk told us they used to
wade across and explore the island after school. Today, this tidal

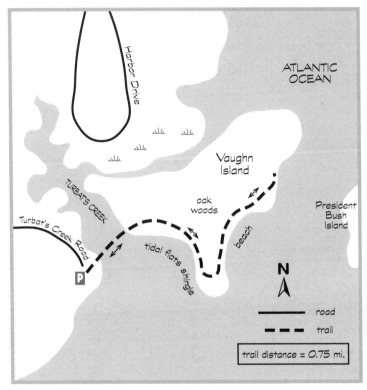

Vaughn Island Trail

island is preserved by the Kennebunk Land Trust for everyone to enjoy.

Children should be with an adult who understands tidal charts and the importance of "time and tide." Depending on the height of the tide on the day of your outing, you'll have about one hour on each side of low when Turbats Creek is shallow enough to wade across.

We recommend wearing high rubber boots or rubber-soled beach shoes; the beach on the other side is rocky. And wear a watch. Vaughn Island has many treasures, and if you lose track of time, you could be marooned for twelve hours waiting for the next low tide to walk back across the channel.

Arrive thirty to forty-five minutes before the low tide for the day you are walking out to the island. Double-check to make sure your tidal chart is specifically for the Kennebunkport area. (Local newspapers and chambers of commerce distribute tidal charts.)

As you face the island, follow the boat-launch road leading to a few boathouses on Turbats Creek. Look for the shallowest crossing to the island on the other side of the creek. If water is above your ankles, don't cross. Gulls, herons, and other waders stand in the bed of this tidal river waiting for the tide to turn and bring in their fish supper.

As you cross the creek, you're likely to see wide "rubber bands" of kelp 5 to 6 feet long and clumps of mussels on the riverbed. Identified by their dark blue-silver shells, blue mussels use threadlike byssal hairs on their shells to attach themselves to pebbles, rocks, and even mud flats (if there are rock particles beneath the surface). Mussels are hardy here—and abundant.

Walk from the "intertidal zone" along the tidal marsh bank on your left and head toward the forested island. Watch your step as you negotiate the wet rocks. In the lower tidal zone, rocks are covered with bladder wrack (rockweed) and can be slippery.

On the other side of Turbats Creek, common periwinkles grow in abundance. These small snails (considered a tasty appetizer in France) migrated to our shores in the nineteenth century. The mainstay of these herbivorous mollusks is algae, which they scrape off rocks and into their mouths with a sort of scouring tongue called a radula. So that they don't dry out between tides, periwinkles glue themselves with a mucuslike substance to rocks and pebbles, withdraw into their shells, and close their lidlike opercula. One of the specialties of these periwinkles (*Littorina littoria*) is that they can extract oxygen to live both in water and in air.

As you climb up the island bank, you'll spot a few rocks with white bands encircling them. During the last ice age when the glacier moved from the Arctic across Maine, the glacier compressed and ground the rock, creating layers of white quartz between green and black granite and shale. Meltwater from the glaciers dumped deposits of these and other rocks at the edge of the ocean. During the seventeenth century, when much of the coast was fished for cod, a smooth, white-banded stone was carried for good luck.

No trail blazes mark the path, but an opening in the oak forest reveals a well-worn path. This path circles the river side of the

Hermit crabs and other marine creatures live in tidal pools at Turbats Creek.

island to the south, and in about 0.2 mile you'll come to a campfire circle with a bench. (Permission is required for overnight camping and fires.) A few yards beyond the circle is the Atlantic side of Vaughn Island. From the Beach, you can see the mouth of Turbats Creek with gulls flying and crying, and, far in the distance, the surf of open ocean. When krill, sticklebacks, and larger fish swim in with the tide, gulls swoop and screech in a feeding frenzy. Ring-billed gulls are common to this area. We also spotted several large black-backed gulls, nicknamed "minister gulls" by early colonists. The wingspan of black-backed gulls measures nearly 3 feet.

Turn left and walk northward along a shingle beach. In summer, a high wall of Japanese honeysuckle borders the oak forest. Along this wall grow magenta-flowered beach peas and three-leaved poison ivy.

At 0.3 mile, a vast tidal marsh of spartina grass separates Vaughn Preserve from the mainland, technically making this an island. A proliferation of burs and poison ivy confines cautious walkers to the beach. Although beachcombing is wondrous, time is of the essence. Remember, you have only about thirty to forty-five minutes after low tide to walk and wade back across Turbats Creek. The island is densely forested; backtrack along the same route.

Once you've safely crossed the incoming tidal water, take time to explore several small offshore islands-in-the-making near the parking area. Silt has been deposited on flat rock ledges, and grass grows around the mirrorlike tide pools. At low tide, coastal settlers often took cows and sheep onto convenient isles like these to graze.

Goose Rocks Beach Walk

Goose Rocks Beach

Cape Porpoise, Maine

Distance: **1.0 mile**
Type of walk: **Out-and-back**
Approximate time: **45 minutes**
Difficulty: **Easy**

A wide, pristine, fine-sand crescent beach overlooking nearby rocky islands, Batson's River, and the Smith Brook estuary.

Getting There

From the intersection of ME 9 and Pier Road in the village center of Cape Porpoise, drive east on ME 9 for 3.0 miles. Turn right onto Dyke Road (to the left, this is Goose Rocks Road) and drive 0.6 mile. Turn right onto Kings Highway and drive 0.9 mile to the end of the road. Four public parking spaces are available near a small circular turnaround.

Special Features

- Audubon piping plover and tern exclosures
- Riparian estuary and 2-mile ocean beach
- Many seabirds on rocky islands just offshore

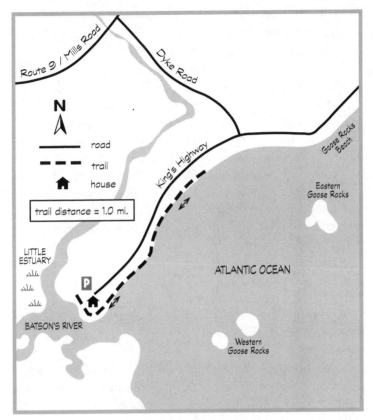

Goose Rocks Beach Walk

This walk has no set markings or blazes. Begin at a Public Way signpost where a short path skirts a private home on the left. This access path leads over a sand dune, past clumps of beach grass and beach peas, to the convergence of Batson's River and Smith Brook. Tidal waters fill this large backwater estuary of grassy hummocks twice a day. The meeting of river and ocean waters in this estuary behind the beach carries valuable nutrients to plants, animals, and birds.

The Batson's River–Smith Brook estuary attracts nesting birds, including swallows that dart and swoop into holes in the silty banks. Most species of small, sleek swallows reside near water in some form—lakes, streams, swamps, and marshes—where they feed on insects. On this end of the beach the swallows fly to and fro from their mud-hole nests in the riverbank.

Curve left around the side of the house, with the river mouth to the right. The Cape Porpoise water tower rises above the coastal forest in the distance. At 0.2 mile, you are walking past private beach property facing the ocean. Please be respectful of private property.

High tide here nearly covers Western Goose Rocks and Eastern Goose Rocks, situated on the ends of this shallow crescent-shaped cove. Low tide transforms the seascape when the long umber-colored rocky islands are exposed at the horizon line. At low tide, this seagull-gray beach of fine sand is perfect for walking.

Beachcombing can be fun, especially for children. One of the most common rockweeds is bladder wrack, a brown, slippery seaweed with air pockets or bladders that keep the sea plant afloat to absorb enough sunlight for photosynthesis. Children can identify the common bladder wrack, washed ashore from the rocks in the cove. (The balloonlike air bladders are fun to pop.)

Clamshells are another beach item children can hunt. They belong to the Bivalve family (shells with two halves). Clams filter water for nutrients. Two main (and Maine) clams that live in intertidal sand zones are the 3-inch, soft-shell clam ("longneck steamer clam") and the 4-inch, hard-shelled quahog ("littleneck clam"). Both are used in clam chowder.

The beach also is littered with carapaces of crabs and blue mussel shells. Blue mussels cling to rocks and pier pilings with strong byssal threads. These filter feeders are strong enough to survive very cold and hot temperatures.

Black-backed gulls likely will fly overhead and are identified by their stark black-and-white coloring. The wings of the greater black-backed are midnight black and measure nearly 3 feet from tip-to-tip, their bodies white. The lesser black-backed, with yellow legs, is similar in size to the herring gull.

In 250 yards, watch for a posted Restricted Area. This is a designated nesting area for 9-inch least terns and 7-inch, pale sand-colored piping plovers. This Audubon-maintained "exclosure" with orange fencing is designed to keep people out. The exclosures also protect nest eggs from marauding skunks. The Audubon Society oversees the progress of the nests, which are protected by Maine and federal laws. A local woman told us she hadn't seen many terns, but the plovers on the beach have done well and produced fledglings.

In addition to least terns and plovers at Goose Rocks Beach, "mud" swallows build nests in the banks of Batson River.

Look for plovers to fly from their nests to the water's edge—but look hard. Their tan-and-white plumage blends with the surrounding sand, and their grass nests are difficult to spot inside the exclosures. In the air these small, quick birds with sharp-angled wings catch the eye, and their high, sharp whistle is a sure giveaway.

No beach is complete without the ubiquitous amphipods, the tiny creatures with two sets of legs, one set adapted for land walking, the other for swimming. You know these irritating little swarms as sand fleas, beach hoppers, or beach fleas. Technically, they're gammarid amphipods. They feed on the algae on seaweed and aid in the decomposition of tidal flotsam and jetsam. When you walk near gammarid amphipods, they fly up like dust. Children will be relieved to know that sand fleas are not real fleas and don't carry disease or cause itching.

Because this cove is relatively shallow, full-moon tides reach farther up the beach. Over the years, storms have occasionally crashed straight through beach houses; some property owners have thus built elaborate breakwaters to protect their property from damaging nor'easters.

As you move down the beach, Timber Island lies ahead, just offshore and can be explored at low tide.

Goose Rocks Beach is about 2.0 miles long. However, when you're opposite Eastern Goose Rocks, you've walked about 0.5 mile. With no public thruway to continue on, return the way you came.

Estuary and Upland Trails

Tyler Brook Preserve
(72 acres)

Cape Porpoise, Maine

Distance: **1.0 mile**
Type of walk: **Loop**
Approximate time: **1 hour**
Difficulty: **Moderate**

A combination of quiet, sparse upland forest wetlands near the Tyler Brook drainage into the Atlantic Ocean.

Getting There

From Cape Porpoise village center, drive east on ME 9 (Mill Road) 1.3 miles to a tidal brook spanning both sides of the road. A small Kennebunkport Conservation Trust sign is posted in the marsh to the right. Just beyond the brook, turn left onto a narrow, unmarked asphalt road. (The access road parallels a private drive and turns to dirt.) Drive 0.2 mile to a parking area on the right indicated by a Kennebunkport Conservation Trust sign. From here, walk the remaining 0.1 mile on the dirt road to the trails.

Special Features

- Numerous wildflowers, including bluets and foamflowers
- Wetlands and upland forest

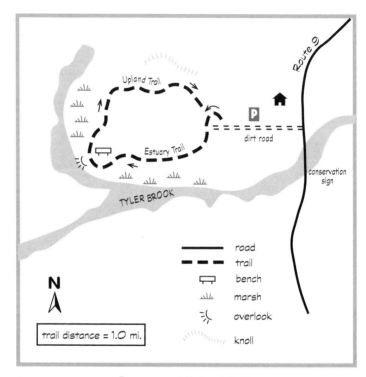

Route 9

Upland Trail

P

dirt road

Estuary Trail

conservation sign

TYLER BROOK

—————— road
— — — trail
bench
marsh
overlook
knoll

N

trail distance = 1.0 mi.

Estuary and Upland Trails

We learned about these trails from a local resident who referred to them as a "well-maintained and well-guarded treasure" of the area. She was right. Meandering inland along the brook, walkers catch glimpses of the marsh through the sparse forest of gray birch, swamp maple, and alder.

Trails are clearly marked with blazes, and a large Kennebunkport Conservation Trust signboard describes the preserve and the trails located within it. Begin by crossing a footbridge over a boggy section and turn left onto the Estuary Trail, following triangular black-and-white blazes. A slat boardwalk protects the groundcover of partridgeberries and lowbush blueberries from tramping boots. Smaller trees yield to larger white birches and give a light, airy feeling to the canopy.

At 300 yards, you come to the first side trail. (All side trails in the preserve are prominently marked with circles.) Keep to the right on Estuary Trail, marked with triangular blazes. To the left, you can see Tyler Brook. Although only a brook, high tide pushes the water downstream into the marsh and riparian open area twice a day. Spring tides (which relate to the full and new moon, not the season) often flood the general area and some of the forest you're walking through. Footbridges on the trail cross runoff ditches and runnels that have left mud and spongy peat areas.

Grass and wildflowers, including the orchidlike magenta fringed polygala (gaywings), foamflowers, bluets, and violets carpet the forest floor. Foamflowers have stalks (up to 12 inches tall) of delicate white blossoms and 3-inch leaves with up to seven lobes on maple-shaped leaves.

At 0.5 mile, Kennebunkport Conservation Trust has placed two benches overlooking the meandering creek. White-tailed deer live in these woods; you might see their hoofprints. And you might catch sight of squirrels, woodpeckers, and other inhabitants while sitting on the bench. This is a nice spot for a picnic, and the benches are cleverly designed so that their backs can be pulled up to form a picnic table. (Just remember to pack out what you packed in.)

Across the brook is a stone wall, a reminder that until about 1930 the seacoast was largely agrarian. Farmers dug drainage ditches and stored salt hay for winter feed in cow barns. Today, active conservation trusts in southern Maine are creating public awareness about the value of tidal marshes, and many marshes that were filled in by dikes and ditches are being reclaimed. At a pair of blue dots, turn right (away from Tyler Brook) and head into the woods on Estuary Trail through a glen of large white paper ("canoe") birches.

Cross through an opening in a stone wall. A side trail comes in from the left, but bear right and continue to follow the triangular blazes. For a short distance, you'll climb whalebacks (smooth humps of granite rock) through a stand of upland white pines.

At 0.7 mile, a little more than midway, Estuary Trail joins Upland Trail, marked with square black-and-white blazes. Turn right, looping back toward the parking area. This section of trail has a decidedly "upland" flavor and skirts a rocky granite knoll in a deciduous forest. Highbush cranberries and sheep laurel get enough light to grow in the well-maintained selective-cut forest. Tree roots have made a network over the path here, so watch your step.

At 1.0 mile, return to the footbridge and dirt access road back to the parking area.

Tyler Brook meanders through a wilderness woodland.

Acknowledgments

The many people who offered their support and interest in this book include: Gayle Kadlik (Star Island), David Powell (Trustees of Reservations), Bill Buckley (Crane Reservation), Jeanne Dewire (Massachusetts Audubon Society), Maggie Redfern (Spencer-Peirce-Little Farm), Carol Decker (Parker River National Wildlife Refuge), Jamie Colen (Fuller Gardens), Sandy Heckman and Brenda Johnson (Sandy Point at Great Bay), Mike Milligan (NH Audubon Society), Arthur Teska (Newmarket Conservation Commission), Sandy Mariner (Wells Chamber of Commerce), Kristi Bryant (Wells Public Library), John Sherman (Kennebunk Parks Department), Tom Bradbury (Kennebunkport Conservation Trust), Doug Rodgers and Jim Dwight (Kennebunk Land Trust), Fr. John (St. Anthony Franciscan Monastery), and Virginia Spiller (Old York Historical Society). Plus the talented AMC Books people—Beth Krusi, Blake Maher, Carol Tyler, Belinda Thresher, and Laurie O'Reilly.

About the Authors

STEVE SHERMAN and JULIA OLDER hiked the Appalachian Trail from Georgia to Maine. They are coauthors of the AMC guides *Nature Walks in Southern New Hampshire* and *Nature Walks in the New Hampshire Lakes Region*. Sherman's mystery novels *Maple Sugar Murders*, *Primary Crime*, and *Highboy* are set in backwoods New Hampshire. In addition to several poetry collections, Older is the author of the historical novel, *The Island Queen: Celia Thaxter of the Isles of Shoals*.

About the Appalachian Mountain Club

Join the Club!

Take a hike, ride a bike, paddle a canoe. We believe that people who enjoy climbing mountains, splashing in streams, and walking on trails have more fun and take better care of the outdoors. Join the fun today. AMC members receive discounts on workshops, lodging, and books.

Outdoor Adventures

From beginner backpacking to advanced backcountry skiing to guided hiking and paddling trips, we teach outdoor skills workshops to suit your interest and experience. Our outdoor education centers guarantee year-round adventures. View our entire listing of workshops online at www.outdoors.org.

Huts, Lodges, and Visitor Centers

The AMC provides accommodations throughout the Northeast so you don't have to travel to the ends of the earth to experience unique wilderness lodging. Accessible by car or on foot, our lodges and huts are perfect for families, couples, groups, and individuals. For reservations call 1-800-262-4455.

Books and Maps

We can lead you to the best hiking, biking, skiing, and paddling destinations from Maine to North Carolina. With more than fifty books and maps published, we're your definitive resource for discovering wonderful outdoor places.

Contact Us

Appalachian Mountain Club, 5 Joy Street, Boston, MA 02108-1490; 617-523-0636; www.outdoors.org

Leave No Trace

The Appalachian Mountain Club is a national educational partner of Leave No Trace, a nonprofit organization dedicated to promoting and inspiring responsible outdoor recreation through education, research, and partnerships. The Leave No Trace Program seeks to develop wildland ethics—ways in which people think and act in the outdoors to minimize their impacts on the areas they visit and to protect our natural resources for future enjoyment. Leave No Trace unites four federal land-management agencies—the U.S. Forest Service, National Park Service, Bureau of Land Management, and U.S. Fish and Wildlife Service—with manufacturers, outdoor retailers, user groups, educators, organizations such as the AMC and the National Outdoor Leadership School (NOLS), and individuals.

The Leave No Trace ethic is guided by these seven principles:

- Plan ahead and prepare
- Travel and camp on durable surfaces
- Dispose of waste properly
- Leave what you find
- Minimize campfire impacts
- Respect wildlife
- Be considerate of other visitors

The AMC has joined NOLS as the sole national providers of the Leave No Trace Master Educator course through 2004. The AMC offers this five-day course, designed especially for outdoor professionals and land managers, as well as the shorter two-day Leave No Trace Trainer course, at locations throughout the Northeast.

For Leave No Trace information and materials contact: Leave No Trace, P.O. Box 997, Boulder, CO 80306; 1-800-332-4100; www.LNT.org